Kingdom and Creation in Social Ethics

by

Chris Sugden

Resident Director, Oxford Centre for Mission Studies

and

Oliver Barclay

Formerly General Secretary of the Universities and Colleges Christian Fellowship

GROVE BOOKS LIMITED

Bramcote Nottingham NG9 3DS

CONTENTS

THE COVER PICTURE

is by Greg Forster with apologies to Michaelangelo's 'Creation of Adam'

First Impression October 1990

ISSN 0951-2667

ISBN 1 85174 161 5

1. INTRODUCTION

by both authors

The following debate results from long term discussions between the two authors and others. In particular the Whitefield Institute convened a discussion group on 'the Biblical Basis of Social Ethics.' Several papers from that group were published in the *Evangelical Quarterly,* Vol.LXII no.1 (Jan.1990).

One of those papers was a statement of basic issues agreed by the group, including the two authors of this booklet. It is important to remember that there are important and fundamental agreements, including the following.

1. Christians have a biblical mandate to be active in society, restraining evil and encouraging all that is good in personal life, and in social, national and international structures and customs.

2. Changes for the better can be made when Christians act together prayerfully and decisively, even if they fall short of the ideal. 'Apocalyptic lethargy' and 'optimistic Chiliasm' are to be avoided.

3. Distinction should be made between what Christians know in ethics, how we know it, and how we argue for it in a mixed society.

4. The group identified these Christian responsibilities;

   i. to witness to the whole will of God, including both evangelism and speaking and acting for God's ideals in society.
   ii. to affirm and speak out for Christian ideals which have their own attraction for many, once understood.
   iii. to exemplify in our lives what we affirm.

A 'Creation' approach to ethics is not the same as 'Natural Law', even if the conclusions of the two sometimes coincide. Nor is CS's use of the 'Kingdom' the same as that of some liberal or charismatic writers. There is considerable diversity in the use of this term.

The aim of what follows is not adversarial. It is an attempt to move forward together. We need a more agreed biblical basis and more agreed terminology derived from it, so that together we can apply biblical themes to our tasks.

At present evangelical writing in this field may agree on practical aims, but be divided over their biblical justification.

2. CREATION AND PROVIDENCE

by Oliver Barclay

When Christians, committed to the authority and sufficiency of scripture, are divided between advocates of 'creation' and 'kingdom of God' approaches to social ethics, one must ask how real their division is. Is the debate merely about slogans? How has the issue arisen?

I believe that the two groups are answering different questions. The 'creation' approach asks about the essential nature of Christian ethics; are they the arbitrary commands of God, the revealed vision of heaven, or the household rules of the church? What is their essence? The 'Kingdom' approach asks how to describe the Christian vision of the ideal society in the here and now. It asks not primarily about the nature of Christian ethics, but about its 'shape' and outworking. Its advocates can be impatient with more fundamental questions and want to get on to the application. It appeals to activists eager to show the immediate relevance of Christian thinking. That concern is right, but until the fundamentals are sorted out it is dangerous to go too quickly to application. In principle, therefore, the two approaches are not alternatives because they work at different levels.

I maintain that we shall not understand or apply correctly many features of biblical ethics unless we recognize that they are essentially based on creation. They reflect the nature of God, creator, providential ruler and redeemer of his creation. That will encompass the ethical features of the valid but ethically more limited concept of the Kingdom of God. To use Oliver O'Donovan's phrase, Christian ethics are 'a reaffirmation of creation'. They are the Creator's instructions arising from his love for the world which he alone understands and brings to restoration and fulfilment.

Only when we have answered the 'ontological' question of the *nature* of Christian ethics can we move to the different, 'epistemological' questions of how we *discover* its demands and how, 'apologetically', we *defend* them. Then also we can address the matter of their *shape* and *practical demands*.

Creation/Providential Ethics

What then is the nature of Christian ethics? Christians of some traditions can give the impression that they are simply and quite arbitrarily God's commands. Speaking of them as 'theonomous' they convey the idea that as God's revealed commands it is improper for us to do more than obey them. Muslims also think their ethics are revealed, while humanists reject all revelation. Thus no space exists for discussing ethical issues with these outlooks, or for persuading them to pursue some joint programme of social amelioration.

Others view the Christian ethical framework as 'voluntarist'. From the ethical supermarket, they say, we have chosen to believe in this product, and are willing to advertise its virtues. Joshua's 'chose you this day whom you will serve . . . but as for me and my house, we will serve the Lord' can be dressed up in these terms.

The Christian cannot be content with either view. Christian ethics is 'obeying the truth', as both Peter and Paul describe it.[1] Christian ethical values are truth, in the sense that this is how we were created to live. They are the God-given programme for living in the world he created and understands absolutely even in its fallen state. He commands what is *best* because he knows what is best, in the double sense that it is both morally right and also for the benefit of humankind because based on the way the world is. It is good, and good for us.[2] Jesus is 'the light of the world' and believers have 'the light of life'. He shows what the world is like and therefore how we should live in it. He came that we should 'have life . . . more abundantly.' That is to say that the Christian way is humanity as it is meant to be. Christian ethics are the 'manufacturer's instructions' for living in his created but fallen world. They thus have an objective foundation in the world as it is. I have argued this elsewhere.[3] The Christian view that God in his revelation has made this provision for the real world implies this objectivity.

Without a 'creation basis' it is difficult to maintain (with Deut.5 and 6, and Ps.34.12-16, quoted in 1 Pet.3) that Christian ethics are best for all humankind.

We are talking of God's order for the world as it is since the fall, rather than in its original state, so it is more precise to speak of creation/providential ethics. The basic creation structures have not changed, but sinful humankind needs restraints while God continues to rule and uphold the world, making arrangements for the fall's consequences. Thus the phrase 'creation ethics' must be understood to include this providence. Hence also the importance of God's law in this providential order.[4]

Thus the New Testament teaching about the place of human authorities arises out of God's providential rule in relation to sin as much as from the original creation—though even in a perfect world there would be decisions to make for good order in society; on which side of the road should one drive, or how should taxes be raised and used, etc.? Creation and Providence merge.

One could illustrate the creational basis of ethics in a number of particular ways. The sabbath was *made for man*. It is a creation ordinance for man's well being. Fornication is a sin against the body.[2] It is an offence against the way we are made. Truth is the basis of much social life. In Ephesians 4.25 Paul says 'let everyone speak the truth with his neighbour, for we are members one of another.' By using the word neighbour he cannot just mean we are members of one another with other Christians in the church. He speaks of society created in such a way that we depend on one another. Truth is vital to good relationships in that community. In Ephesians 4.28 he says that we should not steal, but should work so as to

[1] Rom. 2.8, Gal. 6.7, 1 Pet. 1.22 cf. 1 Pet.3.1.
[2] See Titus 3.8.
[3] See articles in B. N. Kaye and G. J. Wenham (eds.) *Law, Morality and the Bible* (IVP, 1978); and P. Helm (ed.) *Objective Knowledge* (IVP, 1987).
[4] 1 Tim. 1.8-11.
[5] 1 Cor. 6.18.

be able to give to the needy. Work was a creation ordinance for man's benefit, even before the fall[1], with the intention that we should contribute to society. Here and elsewhere the bible gives us creational/providential reasons for obeying God's will as well as telling us that sin is hateful to God and that he will judge it.[2] God's will for humankind is both his holy demand and his loving provision so that we may live in a fallen world as nearly as possible to the way we are created to live. It both *warns* and *rewards.*[3]

By nature, then, Christian ethics are conformity to the Creator's will for his creation, and that is related to the way he has made it, rules it in its fallen state, and sees how it can best operate. The phrase 'creation ethics' arises from this truth. It is not ideal, but it avoids the ambiguities found in phrases such as Natural Law and Common Grace by which people have conveyed *some* of the same ideas.

Oliver O'Donovan, in his magisterial book *Resurrection and Moral Order* writes as follows

> 'A Kingdom ethic which was set up in opposition to creation could not possibly be interested in the same eschatological kingdom as that which the New Testament proclaims. At its root there would have to be a hidden dualism which interpreted the progress of history to its completion, not as a fulfilment, but as a denial of its beginning. A creation ethic on the other hand, which was set up in opposition to the kingdom, could not possibly be evangelical ethics.'[4]

I shall return to the last sentence later.

This creational nature of Christian ethics helps us in other areas also. In *epistemology* we are not left simply with revealed commands, although they should be sufficient for believers. Lying, stealing or hatred are clearly social evils, for instance. They will undermine a happy, healthy society. Almost any society depends on acceptance of this, as non-Christians also recognize. Christian ethics will work and can be shown to work.

We are also helped in *apologetics*. We can argue for Christian standards on a pragmatic basis, without the need to appeal to scripture or to talk about God's kingdom, because we know that God's will is in fact the best, and can demonstrate it. Such an argument is not merely *ad hominem.* It is valid because we believe that God's will is the best. It is not stepping down to lower standards, but pointing to the truth.

The Shape or Outworking of Christian Ethics.

This basic view of the nature of Christian Ethics influences our view of its practical 'shape'. Perhaps we should first note that the New Testament uses several pictures of Christian Ethics, not one universal model.

[1] 1 Gen. 2.16.
[2] Cf. Eph. 5.6.
[3] Ps. 19.11. Note how the OT saints positively love God's law. Ps. 19.10.
[4] I.V.P., Leicester, 1986 p.15.

The *Law* gave Old Testament ethics its shape. Basic negatives, often worked out positively, provided the needed guidelines. The New Testament does not rescind these laws, but interprets them to emphasize not only outward conformity but inward motives and desires, as in the Sermon on the Mount. As an outline the law is not misleading. In Matthew 5 Jesus uses it. In Ephesians 4-6 Paul sets out the Christian life in terms of the Ten Commandments, interpreted on lines similar to the Sermon on the Mount.

But the New Testament refutes any concept of the Christian life as merely obeying rules. One of the ways Jesus expressed this difference was in his teaching about the kingdom of God. This I take to be Oliver O'Donovan's point in saying 'a creation ethic . . . set up in opposition to the kingdom, could not possibly be evangelical ethics.' There cannot be opposition. The kingdom is one way in which the outworking of the creation nature of ethics is expressed in some New Testament passages. Outside a Jewish context the same ideas are usually expressed in other terms: e.g. 'the Gospel', or 'Jesus Christ is Lord.'[1]

The renewal of *the image of God* is one key to the New Testament concept of Christian ethics. Many treatments of the image focus on the Old Testament, underestimating the New Testament references. David Clines, for instance, fails in my view, because the New Testament emphasizes the moral and spiritual aspects of the image, in contrast to the extra-biblical ideas on which he draws.[2]

The New Testament portrays the image of God embodied in Christ, and says we are to be renewed into that image. Colossians 1.15 speaks of Jesus as 'the image of the invisible God,' while Colossians 3.9-11 defines the shape of the Christian life as putting off the old nature and putting on the new, 'which is being renewed . . . after the image of its creator.' The Christian life is seen as renewal of the original creation image, to be seen in the person of Christ.

Likeness to Christ, not a mere set of rules, becomes the Christian ideal. It is a personal not merely a rule concept. Socially the church is seen as his body, and must be a fit 'bride' for him. Nevertheless, without the framework of the law, and the New Testament commands, both positive and negative, this ideal could be sentimentally vague. However, in Colossians 3.12-14, the new nature is given very specific features, culminating with 'above all these put on love, which binds everything together in perfect harmony.' Two general pictures of the Christian life are here put side by side. The restoration of the creation 'image of God' (seen in terms of Christlikeness from ch.1) stands beside 'love which binds all together.'[3] These terms fit with the creational basis of ethics and confirm its biblical nature.

[1] Compare Col. 4.11 with Phil. 4.3.
[2] 'The Image of God in Man', in *Tyndale Bulletin,* 1968.
[3] 'Love has a shape', given specific positive and negative features in this verses. See too Eph. 5.1,2. Thinking of likeness to Christ we must remember that Jesus 'always did his Father's will', and those who love him keep his commandments'. This, in a sentence, answers the situationalist who says there is no command but love.

There are other New Testament pictures of Christian ethics. Despite their closeness to Jesus, neither Peter nor John speak of the Kingdom.[1] Both do speak of likeness to God or Christ. Peter calls us to *holiness because 'I am holy.'* John calls us to be *'pure, even as he is pure'* and *loving, because 'God is love.'* In the Sermon on the Mount Jesus challenges us to be like God in his concern for 'the evil and good . . . the just and unjust.' This is the closest the Sermon comes to social ethics, and it is in terms not of the Kingdom, but of becoming like God.

Galatians similarly, though addressing a problem raised by Jewish opponents, refers to the Kingdom only once in its negative use. The Spirit and his fruit forms its positive outline of the Christian life.

Christian ethics, particularly for a non-Jewish or mixed society, are consistently not presented in terms of the Kingdom. There must be good reasons for this, and to these I now turn.

Shortcomings of a Kingdom Approach

I leave it to Chris Sugden to set out positive reasons for using Kingdom language in social ethics. I have five difficulties with that approach;

1. It is a misuse of biblical terms to apply the Kingdom to a mixed society.
2. It dilutes the bible's challenging gospel of the Kingdom into a new law.
3. It politicizes what is primarily a matter of relationship with God, rather than of ethics, let alone social ethics.
4. Its ethical guidelines are so vague that it can serve almost any political programme. No clear biblical connection is agreed between Kingdom teaching and social ethics. No outline of 'Kingdom Values' for a mixed society is yet agreed.
5. It all too easily seems based on God's arbitrary commands, or to be voluntarist. Many of its supporters therefore bring in 'creation' arguments without seeing how fundamental they are.

1. Misuse of Biblical Terms

The misuse of the phrase 'Kingdom of God' is similar to the misuse of 'Children of God.' The clear New Testament use of the latter is for those who are God's children by new birth. It is not used of humankind generally. Jesus explicitly denies unbelievers the right to call God their father. They are children of the devil.[2] Yet we are tempted to widen the concept to include the whole human race, so losing the thrust of much bible teaching.

The Kingdom of God is not a phrase which appears more than once in the Old Testament, but we are told that *God's rule is now and always over all.*[3] In contrast to idols, he controls history and nature. This 'Sovereignty of God' is undoubtedly a major theme in the Old Testament. Alongside it a distinct *future* kingdom of righteousness, justice and peace, where the

[1] Apart from one future reference in 2 Pet. 1.11.
[2] John 8.39-44, cf. 1 John 3.1-3. Yet public prayers often address God as 'Father of all'.
[3] Ps. 83.1, 96.10, 97.1; and Daniel 4.17, 25, 32.

Messiah will rule, is promised. It is to this future kingdom that John the Baptist and Jesus clearly refer in saying 'the kingdom of God is at hand.' They did not refer to what had always been universally true. We must distinguish the sovereignty of God taught in some Old Testament passages from Christ's messianic kingdom, a Christological concept and a matter of the heart[1] rather than simple obedience to the correct personal or social ethics. As a new lifestyle *for believers* it includes social consequences, but is not primarily about social ethics and is hard to apply to mixed societies.

In the New Testament the Kingdom is Christological and redemptive, requiring new birth even to see it, and personal acceptance of and obedience to Jesus' claims. Promised in the Old Testament its *new reality* is 'at hand' in Jesus, to be entered by belief in him and new birth.[2]

Jesus speaks uncompromisingly of those outside God's Kingdom, whom Paul describes as in the 'dominion of darkness.'[3] Can those in the kingdom of darkness share the activity of God's kingdom? If the Old Testament did not draw so sharp a distinction, or make the inward nature of the Kingdom so clear, then this clarification was part of Jesus' teaching.

As with the phrase 'children of God,' we are rash to widen 'the Kingdom' to include everything that pleases God or is called his sovereign activity. We misuse an important part of Jesus' teaching if we impose Old Testament ambiguity on the New. Jesus clearly intended something quite different. The ideals of the eschatological Kingdom both *inform* social action and *inspire* enthusiasm for what is good for our family, workplace, politics and church, but they are not our main guidelines for the present fallen world.

2. Lack of Definite Social/Ethical Content

This confusion has allowed 'the Kingdom' to become a catch-all phrase to cover anything that is pleasing to God. In a recent collection of papers by 'evangelical social activists' and 'charismatics' it was claimed that the phrase could cover both their different emphases, and indeed, as one of them admitted, it has become so vague that it can recommend policies of both 'Right' and 'Left.'[4]

Thus there is no clear concept of 'Kingdom Ethics.' Is it the ethics of the Sermon on the Mount? If so, does it mean 'resist not evil', go the second mile', 'take no thought . . . etc.?' Or is it a quest for 'Justice in society,' implying political battle, persuading the poor to refuse the second mile and resist evil in asserting their rights? One is fearful that nothing is achieved by using so vague a concept except that our predetermined political strategy is baptized.

[1] As Jesus stressed in the Sermon on the Mount and other teaching in Matthew, leading up to ch. 15.10-19.

[2] John 3.1-16, cf. Matt. 11.11-12 Compare J. Corrie, *Third Way* March 1990 vol. 13 no. 2 p.16. "Wherever God's will is done we may say there the Kingdom is to be seen."

[3] We may distinguish a third use of Kingdom language; the truth of Christ's not yet fully realized 'authority,' (Matt. 28.18, 1 Cor. 15.24-26) well described by M. Schluter and R. Clements in *The Evangelical Quarterly* Vol. 62 no. 1, Jan. 1990.

[4] *Transformation,* vol. 5 no. 4, Oct. 1988 (Paternoster Press, Exeter).

While the Kingdom is the focus of God's will being done on earth, I believe that the Lord's prayer demonstrates that it is only part of that will. Are the phrases 'Your kingdom come,' and 'Your will be done on earth . . .' mere repetitions? If not—and no other petition is duplicated—then 'Your Kingdom come' is a more limited concept than 'Your will be done . . .'[1]

Some features of 'God's will' do not readily come under his Kingdom. Romans 13 shows that God has his ministers of wrath, as well as ministers of the gospel. If the Exodus, and the Return from Exile, are signs of the Kingdom, as often alleged, what of the Captivity and Exile themselves? God's wrath and judgment in society sit uneasily within the Kingdom theme.

Indeed, if 'the Kingdom' is broadened, and so diluted, to comprise whatever is God's will, such as the return of the exiles by Cyrus, or the release of prisoners of conscience by non-Christians[2], where is its Christ-centred nature? Even if Cyrus was 'anointed' for his task, God also 'raised up' the wicked Chaldeans to create the exile in the first place.[3] Are all these Kingdom activities? If so, 'the Kingdom' becomes a vague term not centred on Christ at all, if not, the Kingdom is narrower than God's will. If every 'release of the captives'[4] is taken as a political programme and a sign of the Kingdom, why need Jesus have come at all? Why emphasize that the Kingdom was *at hand* if an unbelieving Cyrus had manifested it years before—or a Gorbachev today? 'Kingdom' ceases to be a Christ-centred concept and becomes a mere political programme, no longer specifically Christian and lacking its eschatological nature.

3. Loss of the New Testament Challenge.

The reduction of 'the Kingdom' to social justice also destroys the personal challenge of the teaching: to live in a righteousness that is not only outward acts, but inward attitudes[5] and to give wholehearted allegiance to the King. If reading the Sermon on the Mount leads only to concern for social justice we have missed the main points of Jesus' teaching. J. H. Yoder's book, *The Politics of Jesus,* seems full of this reductionist treatment of Jesus' teaching, requiring some very strained exegesis.[6]

4. Justice and Righteousness

There is in the literature a frequent mistranslation of the words for 'righteousness' as 'justice.' The broad, 'seek first the Kingdom of God, and his righteousness' is being translated '. . . his justice.'[7] In the context of the

[1] Matt. 6.10. In Matt. 5.45 Jesus says that the impersonal blessings of rain and sun are part of God's will, and no one suggests they are manifestations of the Kingdom.

[2] See G. Cray in *Transformation* vol. 5 no. 4, and C. Sugden *Social Gospel or No Gospel,* (Grove, Nottingham), pp.21, 22.

[3] Isaiah 45.1, Habakkuk 1.6.

[4] As in Jesus' 'manifesto', Luke 4.18ff.

[5] Matt. 5.20, 21, 22, 27, 28.

[6] Eerdmans, Grand Rapids, 1972.

[7] e.g. G. Cray, *op. cit.,* p.27. If he takes righteousness in purely personal terms, one can understand this search for another word. But justice loses all but a particular and limited social meaning, and to narrow Matt. 5.6-11 and 6.33 to justice, as Cray does, is surely unacceptable. There is no evidence that the church of Acts thought they were being persecuted for justice or that social justice should be sought 'first.' When Cray says 'the agenda of the Kingdom may be validly summed up as the restoration of justice and peace,' one must ask, was that all? If so, why didn't they preach it?

Sermon on the Mount it is incredible that the word here means merely justice. Justice is often an aspect of righteousness, but the Sermon is notably about personal righteousness, purity of heart, and putting God first.

From a different theological stable, Prof. Paul Marshall writes, 'if we substitute, *as we should,* variations of the term "justice" wherever we read "righteousness", then the Bible begins to sound quite different.'[1] It will indeed sound different! It will if we substitute any word for the one chosen by the author or swap righteousness for justice the other way round.

It is positively misleading to conflate things that differ, or make a part (social justice) stand for the whole (righteousness). Righteousness is a relationship between God and humankind, and social justice is one between people which may be reduced even to mere politics. The concepts are different, and the main biblical words are different, particularly in the Old Testament where most teaching on social justice is located.

Conclusion

It would be a great step forward in Christian thinking about Social Ethics if we abandoned the use of Kingdom phraseology, and probably also Creation phraseology, when we come to many practical issues. We can then define our ideals, priorities and principles in demonstrably biblical ways. We can then discuss what righteousness means in terms of truth, marital faithfulness, social justice and concern for the disadvantaged on an agreed basis. It would then be easier to set positive aims and attack particular evils in terms of particular biblical themes. This is what the highly successful evangelical social reformers of the last century did, without resort to ambiguous Kingdom language. With plain biblical concern for the disadvantaged, care about exploitation, pornography, education and health they aimed to follow Christ and his example of perfect manhood in seeking 'to do good to all men, especially those who are of the household of faith.' It would be a great gain if we, like them, could go ahead together with *clear* biblical guidelines.

[1] Italics mine. P. Marshall, *Thine is the Kingdom,* 1984, p.53.

3. A PRESENTATION OF THE CONCERN FOR KINGDOM ETHICS

by Christopher Sugden

For 20 years I have debated with Oliver Barclay our common concern to overcome the hesitancy of some western evangelicals to engage in significant bible-based social witness. I stress *westerners,* for such hesitancy is not shared in many parts of the Two-Thirds world where evangelicals have developed their own theology and practice. My own experience leads me tentatively to conclude that one factor underlying this hesitancy is the individual and dualistic categories learned from their culture with which some westerners read the bible. The way forward is therefore not to trade texts, but to examine theologically the framework in which they are understood.

The Kingdom Position

There has been a concern to relate Christian social ethics to the Kingdom of God for the following reasons; practical, theological and biblical.

1. Practical Reasons

If the church is called to invite people to acknowledge the Lordship of Christ personally, it must also exhort them to live out that Lordship in their total life, personal and social. How are personal conversion and social responsibility related? Without a link people become guilty or ineffective, or allow their social involvement to be determined by forces inimical to their faith. Our contention is that personal conversion and social responsibility can only be related through Jesus' Lordship, of which the content is the Kingdom of God.

2. Theological Reasons;

a) Concern for Unity in God's will and activity.

God acts in history and creates a people of God. But human history has been separated into sacred—where God is at work among his people—and secular. The key to uniting them is to regard human history from the perspective of the final Kingdom in which God will fulfil his purpose by the renewal of all creation. In Romans 8.20-21 this renewal is linked with the redemption of the people of God. The completion of God's work in creation is when creation shares in the glorious freedom of God's children.

Therefore the history of God's people is not separate from that of creation. Their freedom anticipates and defines the freedom all creation will enjoy; their history interprets all history, not because God is at work only there, but because there he defines how he works everywhere. And secondly the redemption of God's people must express itself in the renewal of the world, as they demonstrate that their freedom is not for themselves alone, but is a firstfruit of the world's freedom.

b) Concern to discover God's will for Society

How does God intend people to live together in society? What are Christian ethics for human community living, and how should Christians witness to those communities? Many of the issues facing the world and Christians today are social—the role of women in society, sexuality, abortion, race relations, economics, . . .

Some categories by which God's work has been understood divorce God's work in the whole of history from his work among his people, so preventing the development of such ethics. E.g., the use of individualistic categories to describe God's work restricts to within individual believers any true change towards God's purposes for people in society arising from Christ's death and resurrection. From this comes a concern to prove Christians do things best, and that the only way to tackle social evils is to convert people. Hence the world outside the church is viewed as impersonal nature, and the world of persons is focused on the church, for 'God can only work through redeemed persons.' A dualism arises focusing on individual redemption in the spiritual sphere, and as a result some evangelicals are unable to develop a theology for social involvement, which is reduced to changing individuals in their inner lives.

c) Evil overcome through the Cross

Wherever evil is overcome in society it is due to Christ's work on the cross.[1] God's action against evil in any sphere must be related to that victory. Some expressions of evangelical social ethics imply that in some cases God overcomes evil without reference to the cross. This can lead to triumphalism and worldly use of power. But Jesus established the righteousness of God through resisting evil, suffering, death and resurrection. These are the gospel themes of how God redeems the world.

3. Biblical Reasons

God's will is uniquely and supremely expressed in Jesus. Through and for him all things were created, and in him they have their proper place.[2] He is the expression of the Creator, and will bring creation to fulfilment. The focus of Jesus' ministry was the announcement of the Kingdom of God, and that theme gives an overall description of Jesus' work and preaching, and of the work to which he commissioned his disciples.[3]

God's purpose for creation will be fulfilled in his Kingdom, the new age at the end of the world. The life and power of this Kingdom has invaded this age through Jesus. The Kingdom is here in quality, though not yet in its full expression. It is God's gift, and cannot be built by people. In Jesus it fulfils his will for his creation. Its content is rooted in the Old Testament expectation that God would establish his will for Creation—'Your kingdom come, your will be done ...'—forgiveness of sins, new relationships between people, justice for all, a renewed creation and the outpouring of God's Spirit.[4]

Jesus declared that the Kingdom's quality of life was already operative through his ministry; people could now call God 'Abba', Father; a new relationship existed (in his healings) between people and creation, and

[1] See 'Towards a theology of social change,' in R. J. Sider (ed.) *Evangelicals and Development,* (Paternoster, Exeter, 1981).
[2] Mark 1.14; Matt. 4.23; Luke 8.1; 11.20. Matthew uses the phrase 'Kingdon of Heaven.'
[3] Jer. 31.31; Isaiah 35; Joel 2.28-32.
[4] But see Col. 1.12-13; Also Col. 3; 1 Thess. 5.4-6; Rom. 6.5-11; Rom. 8.

between Jew and gentile, slave and free, . . . while the forgiven should also forgive. That ministry continues God's Old Testament revelation, for God's will in Old and New Testaments is one. His will for creation must be understood with reference to its fulfilment in the Kingdom, and to how Jesus demonstrated its life in a world where it conflicted with the kingdom of darkness.

This Kingdom activity is founded in the death and resurrection of Christ: his atonement enables repentant sinners to enter the Kingdom; Calvary defeated evil, enabling people to experience the powers of the Kingdom; the resurrection vindicates Jesus as the one who brought the Kingdom and its newness of life into human history now; it exalts him as Lord, enabling him to give the Spirit. This Kingdom activity is linked with judgment on sin and grace, which is God's activity in opening people to repentance and salvation.

St. Paul does not often use the term 'Kingdom of God'[1], but the concept is there in his theme of the new age, marked by new relationships and the Spirit, invading the old. He focuses on the Lordship of Christ. The Kingdom is about the Lordship of Christ—its key person—and makes no sense without it. The Kingdom centres on Jesus' Lordship and his activity through his people, but it is a fact, dependent not on people's acknowledgement of Jesus. Otherwise if no one acknowledged Jesus, the Kingdom would cease to exist.

Jesus' Lordship is the content of the Kingdom, not Kingdom ethics. Kingdom ethics arise from the acknowledgement of Jesus as Lord of everything. They are not about behaviour in a Kingdom society, nor a blueprint to be imposed legalistically, but are about how people behave who live out Jesus' teaching of the rule of God. They are a response of love to Jesus' Lordship.

A Christian social ethic must be rooted in grace, and related to the good news of the Kingdom announced by Jesus. The proclamation of its forgiveness and new life must be related to the demonstration of that life in new relationships which witness to people's need to give Jesus their allegiance.

When non-Christians express values approximating to Christian values these must be related to the revealed will of God. This preserves the unity of God's actions; his activity inside the church is not separable from his activity outside. Any separation would tend to make church activity irrelevant to the needs God would have his people address in the world. His concern is that all enter his Kingdom; this is the goal of all his activity in the world; all his activity is salvific in intent if not in itself.

The Kingdom integrates the calls to follow Jesus and to steward creation. Paul integrates the two themes by identifying Jesus as the true image of God, the second Adam who fulfils the role of God's image and steward of creation.[2] In the Kingdom of God we follow Jesus in building relationships

[1] In the Genesis account of creation 'image' refers to the human role of dominion over creation. David Clines (*op. cit.*) argues that the image refers to the role of the tenant of an absentee landlord.

[2] Rev. 21.24 speaks about the fulfilment of this role.

of Justice between people and with creation, fulfilling the call to be stewards.[1]

Argument from the Biblical Material

Is the Lordship of Christ, and the activity of his Kingdom confined to where he is consciously acknowledged? Surely not! but his activity where his people are is normative. He does not act in a Kingdom way among his people and in a non-Kingdom way among others. As firstborn both of creation and the new creation he has loved the world, not just his people, and has died to take away the sin of the world. Wherever he acts in the world it is as redeemer and Lord, not just creator. We cannot divide the world into areas where the Kingdom activity is real, and where it is absent. That would undermine Jesus' Lordship over all.

This activity is qualified in a number of ways; first by human sinfulness. Humans do not respond to God's activity. Evil has no future, but continues to exist. Christians are to act in society knowing that evil is dead. Therefore in a sense there is no compromise with evil. Redemption is where the Kingdom is acknowledged and Jesus worshipped, but his Lordship and Kingdom activity also continues beyond those who consciously accept Jesus' rule.

Amidst human sinfulness the only ethics a Christian knows are the ethics of the Lordship of Christ, for Christians have to respond to the absolute. Expediency can always distort because we can never identify how far sin is at work in the pragmatic. If we advocate the pragmatic in a mixed society we say 'the absolute cannot work, so a mixture of absolute and non-absolute can!' How can we know we have the right mixture, leading society up to the absolute good and not down from it?

Amidst sinfulness human society is dynamic, moving up or down. The Kingdom ethic approach recognizes that evil is not static; humanity is involved in a perpetual fall. Even in the best of societies evil remains active. Left to themselves people spiral perpetually downwards. Evil grows inexorably; the counter-activity is Kingdom activity which conserves and lifts creation.

Our Kingdom activity will not convert present society into the Kingdom of God. That will only come when Jesus returns. We simply *witness* to the reality of the Kingdom and the possibility of the absolute—God's intention for humanity—against the distorting witness of evil.

Kingdom activity *empowers* society as Christians and others willing to follow it move in the direction of the Kingdom, counteracting the moral disablement evil brings in society. The Holy Spirit works in society strengthening the wills of people who may not be Christians to turn to God's way.[2] Such empowerment does not guarantee that all will be able to

[1] Rev. 21.24 speaks about the fulfilment of this role.

[2] This trinitarian perspective encompasses the Spirit's work in human community and moves beyond a binitarian perspective involving God and Christ alone.

live out the Christian ethic, but it enables them to see the possibilities and make the choice. Kingdom activity unblinds the masking activity of the evil one, and convicts people, strengthening their wills to act.[1] It conserves society and clarifies people's choice. This makes the invitation of the gospel relevant in every situation.

Without such empowerment society will destroy itself. The world has two options; forwards to God's way, or backwards. Without Kingdom activity what would it look like? Mission fields are replete with examples where Kingdom activity has not just conserved but advanced society. Without it, what would they be like? That is the question to ask, not why everything has not been transformed despite the presence of the Kingdom through Jesus' ministry. Left to itself the world degenerates. Talk of a sense of creation order that God has written into humanity, conserving it and enabling it to acknowledge God and exercise choice, presupposes evil to be other than the dynamic force in people's lives which must needs to be addressed by God's activity in Christ which keeps the choice alive for God. Both evil and Jesus' Lordship are at work in the world; the creation ethics view can become hostage to the view that God is helpless. The Kingdom approach addresses this issue.

Kingdom activity produces *hope.* Its vital eschatological perspective enables active and absolute ideals. Though fulfilment comes when the King comes, the hope is for the present, not just the future. Unlike the intertestamental apocalypses the New Testament does not consign the present to hopelessness. The content of eschatology is the Kingdom—the total Lordship of God, consummating the Lordship of Jesus, and vindicating him, thus fulfilling God's intention for humanity. We can continue in service here because we know we shall be vindicated; we witness to the Kingdom because it will vindicate us. We act, not out of idealism or pragmatic calculation, but because we are convinced that the future will vindicate us. The New Testament people lived convinced that not history but Jesus would vindicate them when he came. We live in the same hope. This is the basis of Paul's argument in Colossians 3; the values Jesus demonstrated, the resurrection vindicated, and which express a risen life hidden in Christ, are eternal; compassion, kindness, humility, gentleness, patience, tolerance and forgiveness.

The Discussion with Non-Christians

We do not impose Christian ethics on a mixed society but converse with people, knowing that the Holy Spirit works to conserve society and enable people to test all laws by these standards and move towards them. No laws are static. They must have a goal. They recognize pragmatic realities but there is a measure and a movement to them. Ethics are relational. They must have movement as well as measure. While we cannot have a perfect society we can move towards one that is closer to a good than an evil one. Without movement forwards we move backwards because of sin. The

[1] This is the argument against the concentration camp guard's line that he is only doing his job.

movement of static rules, which are the lowest common denominator, is always downwards unless an ideal pushes them forwards. Thus some societies have positive discrimination. Equality is not just written into the statute book, but continually maintained.

In discussion with non-Christians the Christian is shaped by all that makes him/her a Christian. Only Kingdom ethics shapes a Christian, for no other represents the Lordship of Christ.[1] When Kingdom ethics is abandoned so is the Lordship of Christ over all aspects of life. That is the beginning of a secularization which declares independence in moral decision-making from external authority, and thus affirms the autonomy of human rule-making. A Christian society and Christian individuals cannot afford to abandon Kingdom ethics as the governing factor in their lives, for this reduces their faith to personal and internal belief.

The motivation for social ethics in Jesus' teaching of the Kingdom is love of the neighbour, integrally linked with love of God. Because of this motivation, Kingdom ethics has no choice but to be available to all neighbours. That is the witness of Christians as they dialogue with non-Christians about how love of neighbour becomes a reality in any society.[2]

If in a mixed society action is based on the lowest common moral denominator, the gospel has no chance. It needs a Kingdom ethic. Anything lower is a secular argument deriving from nineteenth Century liberals who allowed for a general morality in society, and particular moralities belonging to interest groups. At the heart of their argument was acceptance of a lower level of morality for society. Such pragmatism is secular and 'creation ethics' displays such a stance.

[1] Acceptance of dualistic ethics—a Two Kingdoms view—leads to the abandonment of Christian ethics, whereas a Christian cannot abandon Kingdom ethics which is acknowledgement of Jesus' lordship. Two Kingdoms theory allows different laws to apply in the church and the world, and is associated particularly with Luther's approach to social ethics. See *Social Gospel or No Gospel,* (Grove, Nottingham, 1975) p.7.

[2] Take for example the work of the gospel and secular civil servants in India. The gospel enhanced the position of women. Early missionaries such as Charles Grant, motivated by Kingdom ethics talked about gospel standards. Their high Christian vision of the human shaped their values.
They dialogued with non-Christian leaders, lifted people to Kingdom ethics, and prompted reform movements in Hinduism. By contrast the civil servants with a deistic view of God insisted that in a mixed society there can be no appeal to Kingdom 'rules'.
This witness to Kingdom values resulted in two things; gratitude in Indian society for the willingness to witness and refusal to compromise over what men like Grant saw as God's intention for all societies; and Hindu reforms energized by the support of such a movement.
A high Christian viewpoint was being offered, not a pragmatic one. Had they accepted a lowest common denominator, what would that have meant *vis-à-vis* the caste system, or the low place of women? Similarly in South Africa today what denominator can a Christian accept with apartheid, or in Britain with racism?

4. A RESPONSE TO OLIVER BARCLAY

by Christopher Sugden

I do not see the argument as being about Kingdom *phraseology* for ethics in a mixed society. The language can be changed but the underlying concept of the renewed creation, the Kingdom, and the new age relating God's will and redemption to History is fundamental.

Both Paul and Peter, writing to Gentile churches, use such Old Testament images as the new Israel or the holy nation to describe the church, showing that they thought its Jewish heritage important. To argue from a lack of Old Testament background in some readers of scripture is therefore beside the point. What matters is how a Christian social ethic is rooted in the bible, and in Paul's writings Christ's Lordship/the new age is to the fore; this is tantamount to the Kingdom.

I agree with ORB that the Kingdom is over against people in rebellion against God. People have to enter it, and only believers can see it. I do not deny ORB's affirmation that Christian Ethics are rooted in creation, but the Kingdom is the fulfilment of the rule of God the Creator.[1] I do deny that Kingdom ethics are voluntarist or arbitrary, and have never held that view.

ORB suggests that, taken on its own, a Kingdom approach 'all too easily seems based on God's arbitrary commands, or to be voluntarist.' I myself do not take Kingdom ethics on its own in that way. I agree with him about the difference between deriving and defining Christian ethics and promoting and defending them to non-Christians. They are derived from God's will revealed in scripture. I contend that this will is the fulfilment of God's purpose in Creation, expressed in the Kingdom of God.

How we justify Christian ethics to non-Christians will vary depending on what categories they respond to; some cultures appreciate natural laws, or social order; others respond to family issues, and other fundamental relationships.

All find some support in scripture; all derive from a shadowy awareness of God's will, but none is definitive for the nature of Christian ethics. That depends on the definition most adequate to the biblical evidence, and also (as ORB acknowledges) which is most adequate to the fallen state of the world. I suggested the value of Kingdom ethics in this regard above.

I am glad that ORB agrees that 'the Kingdom is one way in which the outworking of the creation nature of ethics is expressed in some NT passages,' and thus affirms the continuity between the two concepts. I should clarify that 'the Kingdom' is not a social programme, nor a set of rules, nor purely about social justice. Nor is it primarily about people's response to God; it is the content of the Lordship of Christ, and its ethics

[1] I agree with Oliver O'Donovan that the 'very act of God which ushers in his kingdom is the resurrection of Christ from the dead—the reaffirmation of Creation', in *Resurrection and the Moral Order,* (IVP, Leicester, 1980) p.15.

are the behaviour of those who have responded in love to Jesus the Lord.

Kingdom ethics may seem vague, but this charge may be levelled at any other biblical material, since we cannot expect to read precise information about every present-day situation direct from scripture. For instance, Christians give the straightforward command not to kill various interpretations in the areas of punishment and war. 'The Kingdom' is not the only biblical concept which is used to support contradictory practical policies; witness the applications of biblical teaching on wealth. The value of 'the Kingdom' is that it draws together the work of God as Creator and as Saviour; his work in persons and in society; the response of faith to Christ and the obedience of faith in discipleship; God's work in the world now and its fulfilment when Jesus returns. It helps counteract the unbiblical separation of these concepts lying behind western evangelical hesitancy about involvement in social responsibility.

I see a distinction in scripture between God's Kingdom activity in the world and people entering the Kingdom. From God's perspective, his Kingdom activity is not limited to leading people to faith in Christ, but can include and use non-believers in so far as their activity promotes his will. Paul appears to affirm this in I Timothy 2.1-6, where he links prayer for kings, proper conduct, and God's will for all to be saved through Christ. The proper activities of rulers can promote God's work of salvation.

ORB argues that if non-Christians can be used in Kingdom activity it is hard to see the new and distinctively Christ-centred dimension of the Kingdom which he stresses. I suggest that he is confusing the objective reality of Christ's Lordship with people's subjective response to it. The Kingdom is new and Christ centred as God acts in history bringing salvation, but all God's people before and after Christ are his people because of Christ. Abraham experienced salvation before Christ; there are signs of the Kingdom apart from God's people and acknowledgement of Christ, but it is still God's acts in Christ which define the Kingdom and have brought it into history.

From the perspective of human response only those who put their faith in Jesus enter the Kingdom. So can God use in his Kingdom activity those who have not yet entered it? ORB properly observes that the Kingdom is Christological. It is Christological because it is the Kingdom of God who is Christ. To deduce that it cannot therefore work through those who do not enter it through Christ is to confuse the objective fact of God's Kingdom and Christ's Lordship with subjective response to it.

How can God's will for mankind be wider than the Kingdom? The Kingdom fulfils God's will in creation. God's blessings of sun and rain do fall on just and unjust, so how do they relate to the Kingdom which people can enter? The classic answer is to divide God's blessings into those of creation (which all share) and those of redemption (forgiveness and eternal life . . .), thus separating these blessings. But in scripture these blessings of redemption are blessings precisely because they transform the blessings of creation—thus in Christ hardness of heart leading to divorce can be cured so that marriage may be fully enjoyed. Blessings of creation do not stand on their own; God's purpose is not that people remain content with temporal blessings, or misuse them, but that they come to worship him.[1] There is a continuity between creation and redemption. As people experience common blessings they may experience them more fully and properly in God's Kingdom.

The confusion may lie in the term 'wider.' In what sense is God's will wider than a Kingdom which is both historical and eschatological? Perhaps people do not enter the Kingdom, or God's blessings for all humanity affect more people than the blessings of the Kingdom which fulfils them, but that does not determine the nature of God's will.

Unbelievers and Kingdom Activity

Is it unbiblical to suggest that social good done by those who have neither repented nor centre their activity on Christ is 'Kingdom activity?' The state of the agents is irrelevant; what matters is that the Redeemer Jesus Christ is Lord over the created order. Biblical evidence is as follows:

a: The New Testament links God's rule in history with that of Christ the ascended Lord.[2] Where just relationships such as characterize Christ's Lordship are established it is appropriate to read them as signs of that rule.

b: Jesus' action and rule are cosmic. He has disarmed the principalities of evil which create division in society.[3] Where we see barriers broken down, can we divorce this from God's will seen in Christ's victory over the powers on the cross?[4] To credit any diminution of evil in the world to any source other than Christ's victory on the cross is to say that some force other than the cross can defeat evil, and thus to undermine the centrality of the cross to God's activity in the world.

c: The 'world' in which the Kingdom is active is both humanity-in-society in rebellion against God, and also a world loved by God. By the cross God overcomes the power of this rebellion; by his love it is not destined for final abandonment but for transformation into a new heaven and earth at Christ's return. In either sense His work is the key to overcoming and transforming 'the world.'

d: Moving from Old to New Testaments we move from law to promise. Redemption, expressed in God's Kingdom, is in fulfilment of his promise and to establish his law. The promise fulfils the law which implied it; they are not separate. The law itself was a gift of grace, fulfilling God's promise of deliverance and of a land where they could serve him. Christ, supremely in his atoning death, fulfils both. Old Testament law, intended to prevent structures from exploiting the poor and to protect and relieve them,

[1] Rom. 2.4
[2] Eph. 1.23
[3] E.g. through the misuse of Jewish law, seen as an elemental spirit in Gal. 4.9
[4] E.g. between Jew and Gentile, slave and free . . . in Gal. 3.28

offered hope not condemnation. It sought to change the status quo, not preserve it, opening it to acceptance of God's promise.[1] Even judgment in society is an expression of grace, as is the Kingdom, pointing people to salvation in the Kingdom and as ORB says a prelude to its coming.

Similarly in the New Testament judgment points towards grace. Judgment separate from grace is condemnation, which must await the last judgment.[2] God works in the political structures in judgment and grace, opening society to conscious acknowledgement of Christ and thus the fulfilment of his purpose for humanity. The goal of this work is always to bring people into the Kingdom. To quote the writer with Vinay Samuel:

> 'We must not identify the action of God's grace in the world outside the church with the conscious acknowledgement of the Lordship of Christ by his believing body. But we do claim that the Lordship of Christ is exercised beyond the church as God acts in judgment and (unacknowledged) grace in the world. The difference between unacknowledged and acknowledged grace lies not in the manner of God's activity but in the nature of man's response. Where men respond to judgment and grace they receive Christ; where men do not respond they incur judgment on themselves.
>
> 'Paul is confident that God works through kings and rulers and the political structures of society to open society up to the conscious acknowledgement of Christ, by judgment on its unjust structures and grace in moving it towards God's purpose for human life. This is the effective operation of the Lordship of Christ in the world beyond the church, to bring creation to its God-ordained goal.
>
> 'This understanding gives a basis for seeing that God is at work in society beyond the church applying the effects of Christ's victory in society through social change.'[3]

The Will of God in a Mixed Society

By the nature of revelation the will of God for a mixed society is found through the reading of scripture by those who accept it, but that will is not for his church only, but for them as the exemplar of what all humanity should be like, as it was with his will for Israel. And his will is not arbitrary, for it is the will of the God who made the created order.

Application of the Sermon on the Mount in a mixed society is not as impractical as some have suggested.

a. We cannot separate Jesus' ethics into ethics for individual obedience and ethics for a mixed society. This separates individual and corporate existence in a way foreign to Hebrew thought.

[1] See especially V. Samuel and C. Sugden, 'Towards a Theology of Social Change' in (ed.) R. J. Sider, *Evangelicals and Development*, (Paternoster Press, Exeter, 1981). A number of issues in the formulation of the views shared in this presentation and response owe a debt to continued discussions with Vinay Samuel.

[2] In Rom. 10 judgment operates on Israel so that Gentiles and Jews may be saved. In 1 Tim. 2.1-4 secular justice provides tranquillity for men to enter God's kingdom.

[3] *op. cit.* p.37

b. To take specific examples; 'Do not resist evil' is not a command for absolute acquiescence, but must be interpreted by Jesus' own practice. He resisted evil by challenging current attitudes to *Torah,* Samaritans, or table fellowship with the *ᶜam ha'arets;* he denounced the Pharisees' hypocrisy, etc.[1]

How does Jesus' renunciation of the sword sit with the teaching that the magistrate does not bear it in vain? After detailed study of Christian pacifism and its alternatives I believe that the nature of Christian love which gives worth to people, founded on God's grace, implies a legitimate form of self-defense applicable in society to the use of force in police action. The nature of Christian love is not self-sacrifice tout simple.[2] Niebuhr's argument that Kingdom love is necessarily self-sacrificial and unworkable in a mixed society has been well refuted by Outka and others.[3]

[1] Matt. 5.39. The alternative Jesus describes is retaliation 'eye for eye.' David Hill in his commentary (*Matthew,* Oliphants 1972) pp.127-128 identifies the context as seeking reparation through the courts. For a fuller treatment see C. Sugden, *A Christian Approach to Violence and Revolution,* (M.Phil. thesis presented to the University of Nottingham, 1974) p.207ff.

[2] See my M.Phil. thesis which was a refutation of this Niebuhrian position, partly on the grounds of the lack of eschatology in Niebuhr's theology.

[3] Gene Outka, *Agape, an Ethical Analysis,* (Yale, 1972).

5. A RESPONSE TO CHRISTOPHER SUGDEN

by Oliver Barclay

Although Chris Sugden and I have discussed over a number of years I do not think he has taken on board my recent analysis that the Kingdom and Creation/Providential approaches relate to *different levels* of the problem. In my view they are therefore not *in principle* alternatives at all. He nevertheless seems to attack a creation approach as if it was the whole statement of the Christian position. In my view it describes an extremely important aspect of the *nature* of Christian ethics, explains why there is considerable convergence with non-Christian ethics and justifies us in believing that Christian ethics are for all people and can often be pursued in cooperation with non-Christians. These points are vital for any social programme. They also bear on the outworking of our ideals. But we need other and more specific biblical instructions to fill out this approach and they will guard against the possible misuses that CS suggests.

Therefore on his first point, 'Practical Reasons', I would reply that the most effective work in this area has been carried out not in terms of the Kingdom, but in terms that can be defended rationally from the discernible creational/providential features of the world. I can discover no signs of Kingdom thinking in the programmes of Wilberforce, the 'Clapham Sect' and Shaftesbury. They and the missionaries whom CS rightly quotes used much more straightforward biblical themes.[1]

Under his 'Theological Reasons' CS argues the need for a theme that unites all God's activity under one head. I do not believe that the Kingdom does this helpfully or biblically. Its attraction is a vagueness which can include everything that you approve of, but, as CS admits, its practical value is small because it is at such a general level. I do not believe we should conflate what ought to be distinguished, even if people call it 'dualism' when you do. Ethical teaching for a *mixed* society does not relate well to this theme and needs other guidelines.

My own view is that the Bible gives us a series of ethical strata of decreasing generality, starting with restoring the creation image—the likeness to Christ, the true image of God. Next we come to holiness, righteousness, and love[2] for God and neighbour (which means all people). Then come more specific commands. Holiness is given a 'shape' in practical terms. The Ten Commandments, as interpreted by Jesus in Matthew 5 and be Paul in Ephesians 4.25—6.9, give us clear social-ethical guidelines, coming down to specifics like truth, not stealing, sexual purity, just wages and honest work, etc. Many of these commands are reinforced in terms of creation/providence, and often can be discerned in general terms by reason.[3] Christians however can stand for them with confidence and

[1] As their diaries show. See for instance: M. M. Hennell, *John Venn and the Clapham Sect,* (Lutterworth, 1958); E. M. Howse, *Saints in Politics,* (Open University and Allen and Unwin, 1952 and Reprints). Diary quotations in S. Meacham, *Henry Thornton of Clapham,* (Harvard U.P. 1964); Also numerous biographies of Wilberforce and Shaftesbury.

[2] See Eph. 4.23 and 5.1-2 for that definition of likeness to God.

[3]. E.g. marriage in Matt.19, unnatural homosexual practice in Rom. 1, and social honesty in Eph. 4. On the role of reason see the essay 'Is there a Distinctive Christian Ethic?' in Basil Mitchell *How to Play Theological Ping-Pong,* (Hodder, 1990). He quotes C. S. Lewis's concept of the 'Platitudes' of social ethics.

clarity as revealed truths. There is no advantage in forcing them into the theme of the Kingdom, especially if that is not primarily about ethics in a mixed society but about the gospel and its outworking *in the lives of disciples.*[1]

The Kingdom approach has difficulty in developing a coherent doctrine of the state, which is crucial in social ethics, or of God's judgments in history. Other aspects of ethics—e.g. marriage and the family, and the environment—seem to present difficulties, but this may be due to a preoccupation with politics.

Finally, though it sounds very evangelical to say 'whenever evil is overcome in society it is due to Christ's work on the cross,' I find it an empty phrase, without biblical basis. CS appears to confuse special grace and 'common grace.' This latter is an ambiguous term, which we have hitherto avoided because the idea of a creation base for ethics is more adequate and biblical. But CS seems in this sentence to try to put everything under special grace. God does of course work through unbelievers, but that results from his general kindness, not from his special grace on the cross. Similarly I do not see where CS finds place for the preaching of the law as well as the gospel.[2] Thus he dismisses the 'two kingdom' approach, which has prompted huge social benefits since the Reformation as well as (for instance) extremely tough opposition to Hitler, giving clear guidelines on the responsibilities and limitations of the state. A Kingdom approach in the last 150 years has never produced a comparably plausible and effective social programme.[3]

Under CS's 'Biblical Reasons' I agree that 'Kingdom activity is founded on the death and resurrection of Christ,' but that does not prove that Kingdom activity is the best way to describe all that pleases God. Scholars find great difficulty in applying the theme to social ethics in a mixed society.[4] Meanwhile a more popular use of the phrase is dangerous, and nothing CS says weakens my criticism of its use to cover all the will of God. With good reason the apostolic writers use other concepts. Even 'Christ's Lordship' is hard to apply to Cyrus and the Babylonian captivity, to 1 Peter 2.13-17 and Romans 13.1-8. Meanwhile Jesus and the rest of the New Testament use 'the Kingdom' for many other essential purposes.

[1] See the paragraph below '. . . Biblical Reasons'.
[2] See 1 Tim. 1.8-11
[3] See quotations given in my article, 'The Theology of Social Ethics; a survey of current positions,' in *Evangelical Quarterly,* vol.LXII, no. 1, 1990. Reformed as well as Lutheran social ethics was shaped by the 'two kingdoms' teaching, e.g. in the Scottish Reformation. Liberal theology had not eroded the force of the 'two kingdoms' approach in Lutheran Norway and Reformed Holland, as it had in Germany, and Hitler's demands were resisted in Norway and Holland by Christian believers as almost no-where else, and for theological reasons. See also Brian Stanley's article in the same volume of *E.Q.;* 'Evangelical Social and Political Ethics: an historical perspective.'
[4] See e.g. G. E. Ladd, *Jesus and the Kingdom* (SPCK, 1966), where out of 335 pages he can devote only two to social ethics and those are indecisive. See other works by Ladd and also J. D. G. Dunn, (ed.) *The Kingdom of God and North East England,* (SCM, 1986); Bruce Chilton and J. I. H. McDonald, *Jesus and the Ethics of the Kingdom,* (SPCK, 1987); G. Beasley Murray, Jesus and the Kingdom of God, (Eerdmans, 1985), and R. T. France, *Divine Government* (SPCK, 1990).

Henri Boulad

Dimensionen der Liebe

Henri Boulad

Dimensionen der Liebe

Persönliche Aufzeichnungen

Übersetzt aus dem Französischen
von
Hidda Westenberger

Edition Tau

Imprimi potest Provinzialat der Gesellschaft Jesu
Wien, am 4. 10. 1988

Übersetzt aus dem Französischen von Hidda Westenberger
Umschlagentwurf: Gerri Zotter
Druck: A. Luigard Ges.m.b.H., Wien

ISBN 3-900977-10-0

Inhalt

Brief an eine junge Verwandte

Heute feierst Du Deinen 19. Geburtstag, und ich möchte Dir sagen, daß ich soeben während meiner Morgenmesse ganz besonders für Dich gebetet habe. Und noch etwas: Mit diesem Brief möchte ich gern unsere heiße Diskussion fortsetzen, die uns beide neulich bei Euch gepackt hatte.

Zunächst einmal mein Dankeschön, daß Du mit solcher Offenheit und Aufrichtigkeit geplatzt bist! Das hat Dich und mich befreit. Ich mag es gern, wenn man gewisse Dinge, die einem in der Kehle stecken, frank und frei heraussagt, um sich darüber auszusprechen – mit den andern. Das ist wichtig. Wenn ich es selber tue dann und wann, dann geschieht dies gewöhnlich wohl zu kraß, was Du mir ja auch heftig vorgeworfen hast. Erlaube mit bitte, mich etwas zu erklären.

Meine Art zu lieben ist anspruchsvoll zu sein, sehr anspruchsvoll sogar. Die Liebe mag als milde Schonung verstanden werden oder als strenge Forderung, und ich habe die letzte Art gewählt, den Anspruch gegenüber dem anderen. Für mich bedeutet jemanden lieben, ihn größer haben zu wollen, ihm dabei zu helfen, aus sich auszusteigen und über sich hinauszuwachsen. Liebe bedeutet für mich, den andern auf besondere Weise zur Selbstüberwindung herauszufordern.

Weil ich Dich liebe, weil ich Euch alle liebe, weil ich Deine Cousins und Cousinen liebe, und weil ich die alexandrinische Jugend liebe, deshalb richte ich ein unmögliches Ideal vor Euch auf. Doch lies diesen Spruch, den ich sehr mag:

> Nicht der Weg ist das Unmögliche,
> sondern das Unmögliche ist der Weg.

Eine Forderung des Unmöglichen kann als absurd gewertet werden, das Ziel ist unerrreichbar, und so bleibt es eine Forderung großer Härte. Wenn man aber in diese Richtung schaut, dieses „unmögliche Ziel" ernst nimmt und trotzdem mutig drauf zugeht, dann gibt es zumindest etwas zu ernten: Man wird innerlich auf diesem Wege wachsen! Ich würde Euch betrügen, wenn ich Euch schmeicheln würde mit lauter süßem Gerede, und wenn ich Euch dort stehen ließe, wo Ihr steht. Nein, ich will Euch höher reißen, ich will Euch wachsen sehen, ich will Euch groß haben! Das ist halt meine Art, Euch zu lieben.

Dein Leben und das Leben der heutigen Jugend im allgemeinen ist mir viel zu bequem geworden, es lebt sich zu leicht. Dabei geht Ihr das Risiko ein, am ernsten und heroischen Aspekt des Lebens vorbeizuleben. Es ist nicht Dein Fehler, wenn Deine Eltern es sich leicht machen und Dir ständig alles bieten. Diese Wohlstandsbequemlichkeit als neues Ideal birgt jedoch ein schlimmes Risiko, denn Eure edlen Kräfte schlummern ein oder werden nie geweckt.

Tadle mich deshalb nicht, wenn ich Dich gelegentlich aufschrecke und provoziere, wie ich es auch des öfteren in meinen Predigten und Vorträgen mit den Zuhörern tun muß. Damit richte ich sie nicht, und ich richte Dich nicht, ich richte niemanden, und noch weniger verurteile ich jemanden. Aber ich sehe, daß Gott Dir überreichlich gab und gibt, Dir, Deiner Familie, Deinen Verwandten und all Deinen Freunden, sodaß ich maßentsprechend gewisse Forderungen an Euch stelle.

Das dürft Ihr bitte nicht mißverstehen und es mir als Liebesmanko ankreiden, denn es ist gerade das Gegenteil. Meine Zuneigung für Euch würde wenig taugen, wenn Sie darin bestünde, Euch zu schmeicheln und nur zu schmeicheln. Oh, es fiele mir nicht schwer, Euch lauter hübsche Dinge zu sagen und nichts weiter.

Für die Mehrzahl der Menschen besteht der Liebesbegriff in blumigem Tun und Reden und in einer endlosen Nachsicht gegeneinander. Aber es gibt noch ein anderes Gesicht der Liebe, das des strengen Forderns und Bemühens umeinander. Natürlich ist dieses Gesicht ernster, zweifellos aber wahrer. Es ist ernst und wahr, weil es zur Selbstüberwindung reizt und zum Wachstum treibt.

Jede Geburt ist schmerzvoll, die Geburt unseres wahren Ichs ist vielleicht noch schmerzvoller als die erste zu Beginn unserer Existenz. Ich-Werdung ist Ent-bindung, also eine Entbindung wie bei einer leiblichen Geburt. Bitte träume niemals von einem süßen und allzuleichten Leben, sondern von einem heroischen, einem „unmöglichen" Leben, denn nur ein solches Streben wird Dich glücklich machen können. Du machst die Erfahrung eines ganz anderen Glücks als das des Wohlstands und der „netten Stunden", der starken Komplimente und des schnellen Erfolgs. All das ist Lüge! Täusche Dich ja nicht, ein Teil unserer Gesellschaft lebt in dieser ständigen Lüge; man heuchelt in allen Regenbogenfarben und beschenkt sich hin und her, und was ist hinter dieser schönen Fassade? ... Ich gehe dieser Form menschlichen Beisammenseins möglichst aus dem Wege, und damit gehe ich der Lüge aus dem Wege. Wenn ich doch einmal hineingezogen werde, dann bin ich sehr offen und vielleicht zu scharf, Du hast ganz recht!

Ich hab' Dir weh getan. Wirst Du mir es vergeben? Werden die Alexandriner mir meine zu „absolute" Predigtsprache auch vergeben? Ich hoffe doch, daß sie mich verstehen und wissen, daß es keineswegs Verachtung ist, sondern das Gegenteil: Achtung vor ihrem wahren Menschentum.

Wenn ich fühle, daß irgendwo versteckte Möglichkeiten schlummern, daß eine potentielle Energie bereitsteht, aber ungenutzt bleibt, dann muß ich sie provozieren. Die Alexandriner haben in der Nächstenliebe schon viel gegeben, und sie werden weiter geben. Du auch! Du hast ein goldenes Herz! Ich würde es nicht zulassen, daß dieses Herz in einem falsch gelebten Dasein schrumpft und daß es sich mit dem üblichen Spaß am Leben schon begnügt, nicht zu vergessen unsere Mode-Tyrannei und die infantile Überschätzung ihres Wertes ...

Unzählige Menschen um Dich her, und nicht nur in Ägypten, erhoffen von ihren Mitmenschen, denen es besser geht, ein wenig mehr Freude, sie sehnen sich nach ein wenig mehr Liebe in Wort und Tat. Es gibt so viel menschliche Tragik. Woher nehmen wir uns eigentlich das Recht, unsere ideellen und materiellen Schätze zu hüten und nur zu unserem eigenen Nutzen auszukosten? Welche Eigensucht und welche Trägheit! In jeder Hinsicht sind wir sehr verwöhnt worden. Man braucht daher kein schlechtes Gewissen zu haben, aber man muß ganz einfach erkennen, daß diese „Talente" uns nicht gegeben wurden, um sie zu „vergraben", sondern um sie in unserer Umwelt nutzbringend anzuwenden.

Vielleicht tust Du schon Dein Möglichstes? Vielleicht gibst Du bereits anderen, soviel Du kannst? Ich weiß es nicht. Diese wichtige Frage mußt Du Dir ganz allein stellen und beantworten, denn von der Antwort hängt der Wert Deiner Existenz ab.

> Der berauschendste Augenblick im Leben eines Menschen
> ist der, wenn er erkennt, daß er gebraucht wird.
>
> (Paul Claudel)

> Es gibt keine größere Freude und kein größeres Glück
> für den Menschen, als sich ganz an etwas hinzugeben.
>
> (Marcel Légaut)

Dieses Ganze ist mein Wunsch für Dich und für die Jugend Alexandrias. Gewiß wird dieses Ganze für jeden ein anderes Maß haben, objektiv gesehen, weil es keine zwei Wege gibt, die einander gleichen. Wichtig ist allein, daß der einzelne seinem Leben ein Höchstmaß an Liebesengagement und Selbsthingabe abverlangt. Wie anders sähe die Welt aus, wenn dies schon das Ideal der Mehrzahl oder gar aller wäre! ... Ich versuche es zumindest zu proklamieren. Vielleicht gehe ich dabei manchmal ungeschickt vor, ja zu direkt. Möge man mir das vergeben. Aber ich träume so sehr von einer neuen Welt und sehe, daß der Herr uns genügend innere Kraft und unendliche Möglichkeiten gab, damit wir diese in jeder Hinsicht notleidende Welt in eine Welt der Liebe wandeln. Alles hängt von uns ab, vom einzelnen!

Daß mein Schrei auch der Deine wäre! Daß mein Appell auch der Deine wäre! Meine Stimme ist hier ein Ruf in der Wüste, daher brauche ich Mit-Stimmen und Mit-Rufer, damit die Revolution der Liebe auf unserem Planeten sich ausweite und Wellen schlage. Ich glaube daran. Ich glaube, daß diese Revolution keine Utopie ist. Mein ganzes Leben habe ich bisher dafür eingesetzt, aber ich brauche Mitarbeiter! Das Echo vieler ist bereits großartig, aber ich will noch mehr, viel mehr! Daher gehe ich betteln, daher werbe ich um einsatzbereite Herzen, daher fordere ich in dieser Strenge. Es brennt ein Feuer in mir. Ob Du es fühlst?

Dabei weiß ich recht genau, welche Belästigung und unangenehme Herausforderung mein Anliegen bedeutet und daß es die Menschen in Verlegenheit bringt ... , aber das ganze Evangelium ist eine

Belästigung sondergleichen! Der erste, der seine Mitmenschen in dieser Weise belästigte, war Christus. Daher hat man ihm den Mund verboten und ihn an ein Sterbekreuz geschlagen. Das Evangelium ist eine sehr unbequeme Sache, es ist sogar unerträglich für die meisten! Doch kommt niemand an ihm vorbei, niemanden kann es wirklich gleichgültig lassen, es provoziert jeden von uns, es ist die Herausforderung par excellence.

Ja, Christus hat die Menschen belästigt. Und die Liebe, die er uns brachte, hat keine bonbonrosa Farbe, noch einen solchen Geschmack, noch lullt sie uns ein in selige Träume. Nein, es ist eine Liebe so rein und hart wie ein Diamant.

Ich bin gekommen, Feuer auf die Erde zu werfen,
und wie sehr wünschte Ich, es loderte empor!

(Lukas 12, 49)

Glaubt nicht, Ich sei gekommen, Frieden in die
Welt zu bringen. Nicht den Frieden wollte Ich
bringen, sondern das Schwert. Ich bin gekommen,
den Sohn mit seinem Vater zu entzweien, die
Tochter mit ihrer Mutter, die Schwiegertochter
mit ihrer Schwiegermutter.

(Markus 10, 34-35)

Glaubt Ihr, Ich sei gekommen, Frieden in die
Welt zu bringen? Nein, vielmehr Entzweiung!

(Lukas 12, 51-52a)

Wenn es nicht anders geht, dann eben durch Feuer, Schwert und Entzweiung. Christus und das Evangelium sind Zeichen des Widerspruchs, und alle diejenigen, die sich auf ihn und sein Wort einlassen und auf das Evangelium berufen, werden zwangsläufig selbst zum Zeichen des Widerspruchs. Unvermeidbar! Christus bedeutet immer eine aufsteigende Kraft, und jede aufsteigende Bewegung steht den Gesetzen von Gewicht und Masse konträr entgegen. Wie soll sie ohne Opposition ihren Kurs nehmen können?

Ich breche hier ab, mein Liebes, dieser Brief war in dieser Länge gar nicht vorgesehen. Ich bedaure keineswegs unsere Auseinandersetzung, die wir hatten, im Gegenteil, sie geschah ganz gewiß im

Zeichen der Gnade. Ich rechne fest damit, daß diese Offenheit zwischen uns bestehen bleibt, selbst um den Preis gelegentlicher Schmerzen. Diese aber fördern uns im Steigen, und wir müssen steigen; sie helfen uns bei Wachstum und Veränderung, damit wir ein wenig mehr von dem werden, was der Herr von uns erhofft. Das Ganze ist ein Weg ohne Ende, das Wesentliche ist, sich für ihn zu entscheiden – und zu starten.

Bete für mich wie ich für Dich, daß der Herr uns helfen möge, mehr Liebe in unserem Leben zu entfalten und sie dorthin zu tragen, wo sie gebraucht wird. Möge sich ein neues Herz im Menschen regen ...

Umarmung! Und verzeih mir, daß ich Dich verletzt hatte.

Dein Onkel Henri, der Dich liebt.

Original in Französisch
(Alexandria/Ägypten 1982)

Vom Eros zur Agape
Die Logik der Nächstenliebe

Durch die Lust und Freude am Vergnügen, durch das Sehnen und Verlangen steuert Gott alle seine Geschöpfe und bewegt sie von innen her. Unser Bedürfnis nach etwas, dieser heftige Wunsch, es zu erlangen, stellt jenen Instinkt dar, der uns antreibt, fortwährend etwas zu wollen und das zu wählen, was uns am besten dient, d.h. was unser Bedürfnis befriedigt. In der Natur eines lebenden Wesens entspricht jedes Sehnen einer Notwendigkeit, einem Durst, der, wenn er gestillt wird, für eine Weile Glück und Wohlbefinden erzeugt. Das ist das Gesetz der Natur, wie Gott es erdachte, das ist unsere innere Führung, das ist der unbewußte Trieb aller Wesen. Somit liegen Norm und Richtung unserer Lebensgeschichte in uns selbst.

Wäre das aber alles, dann wäre der Mensch grundsätzlich ein animalisches Wesen; wie soll sich dieses egoistische Bedürfnis jemals zur Nächstenliebe entfalten können? ...

Die Materie ist perfekter Egoismus. Erst mit dem organischen Leben und der Zellteilung leuchtet in der Welt der erste Funke von „Nächstenliebe" auf, denn das Wesen, das sich teilt, verzichtet auf seinen alleinigen Selbstbesitz. Die Sexualität, eine Stufe höher, ist schon Hingabe und Austausch, hier zeigt sich bereits eine deutliche Tendenz zur Nächstenliebe. Ohne Zweifel ist dabei noch jeder Impuls von Egoismus durchtränkt, doch finden wir hier bereits ein Suchen und Tasten nach etwas anderem.

Bei genauer Betrachtung enthält die Erotik tatsächlich ein gewisses Selbstvergessen im Hinblick auf den eigenen Genuß. In der sexuellen Liebe wird das Glück des anderen angestrebt als Voraussetzung zur eigenen Erfüllung. Demnach ist er zwar noch immer Egoismus, doch ein Egoismus auf gehobener Stufe oder feineren Grades, denn er kündet von der Nächstenliebe und lockt sie herbei. Die Erotik ist ein Köder an der Angel Gottes ...

Ähnliches geschieht fortwährend in unseren gesellschaftlichen Beziehungen. Man liebt, man hilft einander, man schätzt und respektiert jemanden, um selbst geschätzt und respektiert – und vielleicht geliebt zu werden, kurz, um die Aufmerksamkeit auf sich zu lenken und die anderen zu gewinnen. Hier stehen wir an einer Schwelle, denn ein weiterer wichtiger Schritt muß getan werden:

Wir erkennen, daß unser vollkommenes Glück erst darin bestehen wird, vorrangig die anderen glücklich zu machen. Auch die Freude von Mutterschaft und Vaterschaft gehören hierher. Wir werden froh am Glück der andern, das Mit-Erleben ihrer Freude erhebt unser Herz. Auf dieser Stufe angelangt, fragen wir uns, ob wir die wahre Nächstenliebe üben. Legen wir bei der Antwort den Maßstab an den Paulus-Text des Hohen Lieds der Liebe:

Die Liebe ist langmütig,
die Liebe ist gütig,
sie ist nicht aufgeblasen,
sie ist nicht prahlerisch,
sie sucht nicht den eigenen Vorteil ...

Sie freut sich über die Wahrheit,
sie erträgt alles,
sie glaubt alles,
sie hofft alles,
sie übersteht alles.

(aus I Korinther 13)

Wir gingen aus von der Lust und Freude am Vergnügen und haben uns schrittweise zur reinen Nächstenliebe erhoben. Das ist die göttliche Führung und unser innerer Wegweiser. Auf der Suche nach der eigenen Glücksbefriedigung führt Gott uns zur Liebe und über die Liebe zur Nächstenliebe. Wir gehen den Weg vom Eros zur Agape, denn eines Tages entdeckt die Selbstliebe, daß sie sich zur All-Liebe entfalten muß.

Du sollst Deinen Nächsten lieben wie Dich selbst.

(Matthäus 19, 19b)

So steht also die Eigenliebe an der Wiege der Nächstenliebe? Welch bewundernswerte Pädagogik Gottes in unserer Welt! Weit entfernt davon, unverständlich oder gar unsinnig zu sein, ist die Nächstenliebe tief in die innere Logik des geistigen Wesens eingeschrieben. Jeder rechtschaffene Mensch, wahrhaft gegen sich selbst und seiner Natur treu, wird dieses fest in ihm verankerte Gesetz als das Gesetz seines persönliches Wesens erkennen.

Originaltitel:
L' Evolution d' EROS vers AGAPE ou la logique de la charité
(Beirut/Libanon 1961)

Die Vereinigungstendenz des Seins

Am Ursprung der Dinge finden wir die vollkommene Identifizierung von Materie und Energie. Es ist das große Verdienst der modernen Wissenschaft, uns diese Gleichsetzung offenbart zu haben, denken wir z.B. an Louis von Broglies Nachweis der Materiestrahlung und an den nachfolgenden Begriff der „Broglie-Wellen". Andererseits erkennen wir im Herzen dieser Ur-Einheit zwei gegensätzliche Pole: Das Positive und das Negative umklammern und verbinden sich zu etwas Unauflöslichem. Dies nenne ich den in der Materie fest verankerten Egoismus.

Mit dem organischen Leben und der Zellteilung erscheint das erste Phänomen einer Teilung, einer Aufteilung, einer Nicht-Identifizierung. Doch zur selben Zeit dieser Trennung erscheint auch hier im vollen Gegensatz dazu das Phänomen der gegenseitigen Anziehung dieser geschiedenen Elemente. Es ist der sexuelle Trieb. Die Sexualität strebt in ihrem Paarungsbedürfnis zu einer Wiederherstellung der verlorenen Ur-Einheit.

Der sexuelle Weg bleibt jedoch ein Kompromiß. Zeichen dafür, daß die Einheit, auf dieser Ebene vollzogen, noch keine ausreichende ist, gibt die Fortpflanzung, die in die Schaffung eines neuen Wesens mündet, das sich zwischen die beiden Paarungselemente stellt. Dieses dritte Wesen ist die lebende Verneinung jener Möglichkeit, daß ein Paar auf sexueller Ebene zur vollkommenen Einheit gelangen kann. Die Rolle dieses dritten Wesens aber ist die des wichtigen Wegbereiters des Lebens dieser Erde zur Entfaltung in der Nächstenliebe.

Bereits im Tierreich ist der Ruf zum Aufstieg auf ein höheres Niveau wie ein Appell zum Transzendieren zu finden, d.h. eine Einheitssuche, die unaufhörlich alles Biologische und Sexuelle überschreiten will. Inwiefern? Weil der sexuelle Trieb im Tierreich zur Entwicklung des elterlichen „Liebesinstinkts" für die Nachkommenschaft führt.

Das erste Ergebnis der Zeugung ist demnach in Andeutung bereits beim Tier Nächstenliebe. Der Baum bringt seine Früchte hervor und läßt sie unbekümmert fallen. Viele Tiere dagegen setzen ihre Kleinen in die Welt und verlassen sie nicht, bis sie sich allein zu helfen wissen. Noch im Ei behütet und bedeckt die Mutter sie bis zum Ausschlüpfen. Natürlich leugnen wir nicht, daß es Tiere gibt, die ihre Eier ablegen und vergessen. Bedenken wir aber, daß solche Tiere zu den niederen Arten gehören (Fische, Reptilien), die dem Egoismus, von dem wir sprachen, noch näher verhaftet sind.

Mit der Evolution der Arten erleben wir ein in seiner Qualität fortschreitendes Sorgetragen der Eltern für ihre kleinen Wesen, die sie gemeinsam hervorbringen. Bei höheren Formen, die zum Menschen führen, gibt sich die Mutter nicht mehr damit zufrieden, die Jungen zu säugen, sondern sie liebkost und umarmt sie, sie drückt sie an ihr Herz.

Man könnte sich fragen, ob die Entwicklung der Hand, charakteristisch für den Aufstieg zum Menschen, nicht auch Ergebnis dieses mütterlichen Instinkts ist, der die Jungen an sich schmiegen und schützen will. Zudem führt diese Geste in ihrer ständigen Wiederholung, besonders beim Herumtragen der Jungen, das Tier langsam zur aufrechten Haltung, die den Menschen ankündigt. Das ist eine Hypothese. Welche Folgen diese Geste in der Evolution der tierischen Morphologie auch haben mag, eines ist sicher: Der elterliche Instinkt will innerhalb des evolutionären Aufstiegs hervorbrechen und sich entwickeln.

Mit dem Menschen erreicht dieser Instinkt eine neue Stufe, die der bewußten Nächstenliebe. Wohlverstanden, der Mensch hat noch Teil am tierischen Wesen, aber alles, was wir über die Funktion und das Ergebnis der Sexualität bei den höheren Tierarten gesagt haben, gilt nun auch für den Menschen. Ganz wie beim Tier wird die Rolle des kleinen Kindes für die Entwicklung des menschlichen Elternpaares entscheidend sein, denn das Paar erreicht jetzt eine höhere Qualität als die der rein physischen und sexuellen Vereinigung. Das Kind ist die Verneinung des Egoismus für beide Elternteile. Das

Kind zwingt die Liebe der Eltern, sich auf eine höhere Ebene zu erheben, die Ebene des GEBENS, des SICH-GEBENS. In dem Maß das Kind aufgenommen, angenommen und geliebt wird, entwickeln sich Familienbande einer ganz anderen Ordnung als die der bloßen sexuellen Vereinigung eines Paares.

Innerhalb des Familienkreises aber sind wir noch immer auf der „natürlichen Ebene", die Familie muß sich bald der Gesellschaft gegenüber öffnen, welche erst der Ort der wahren Nächstenliebe ist. Auch hier ist wieder das Kind das Instrument einer neuen Selbstüberwindung. Die „Brüderlichkeit" unter den Kindern im Nest der Familie ist schon eine Lehrzeit für ihr späteres Verhalten in der Gesellschaft. Dort wird es diese rein familiäre Brüderlichkeit auf sein Schul-Milieu ausdehnen und später auf sein Arbeitsmilieu. In dem Maß die Eltern dieser Bewegungstendenz folgen, sich interessieren, sie gutheißen, in dem Maß werden sie auch ihre engen Familienbeziehungen lockern und den Kreis zu öffnen wissen für die andern.

So ist das Kind das Element, das die Familie veranlaßt, sich zu übersteigen und etwas anzustreben, das außerhalb von ihr liegt: die Gesellschaft. Die Gesellschaft ist berufen, die vollendete Form der Brüderlichkeit darzustellen, sie ist, wie wir sagten, der Ort der Nächstenliebe.

Wieso? ... Weil die Nächstenliebe eine unbefangene, uneigennützige Form von Liebe und Zuwendung ist, die sich selbstvergessend hingibt. Sie will allen Partikularismus von Familie und Verwandtschaft, von Rasse und Nation überschreiten. Die Garantie des Selbstvergessens der Nächstenliebe ruht in ihrem u n i v e r s a l e n Z i e l . Das Kriterium einer authentischen Nächstenliebe ist demnach sein „katholischer" (allumfassender, universaler) Charakter. Sie ist nur in der Gesellschaft möglich. Unter Gesellschaft verstehen wir nicht eine bestimmte Gesellschaft, welche auch immer, sondern wir verstehen „die" Gesellschaft, d.h. die ganze Gemeinschaft der Menschen dieser Erde.

Im Maß des Hinwendens zum „Du" – und hier soll ein Du jeder Art möglich sein – wird Liebe zu Nächstenliebe. Hier vollzieht sich der Schritt vom Besonderen und Einzelnen zum Universalen.

Wohin aber strebt diese Nächstenliebe? Was ist ihr Ziel? ... Ist sie nicht die Verneinung jedweder Einheit, und durchkreuzt sie nicht das starke Streben des Menschen zu einer Reintegrierung seines Wesens? ... Ist „universale Liebe" nicht Zersplitterung des Ichs, Zerfall und Rückkehr in die Vielheit? Liebe zu Nächstenliebe werden zu lassen, heißt das nicht, einen sicheren Vorteil für eine vage Hoffnung zu verspielen? ...

Die Nächstenliebe könnte uns tatsächlich als Illusion und Absurdität, also als Unsinnigkeit erscheinen. Selbstverleugnung zugunsten des andern, warum und wofür? Was ist der Lohn, die Gegenleistung? Wo liegt der Sinn dieses Opfers, denn Nächstenliebe ist ja doch Opfer! ...

Erinnern wir uns, was wir anfangs sagten: Die Nächstenliebe ist in unserer Natur angelegt, der Mensch ist auf sie ausgerichtet, er wird zu ihr hingesteuert. Demnach kann sich der Mensch im Grunde genommen der Nächstenliebe nicht entziehen, ohne zu „sündigen". Die Nächstenliebe ist eine tief in ihn eingeschriebene Wesenstendenz, die tiefer in ihm wirkt als aller Egoismus. Die Nächstenliebe ist für die menschliche Natur eine Notwendigkeit, eine ontologische Forderung, d.h. sie liegt begründet in seinem Sein.

Wohin tendiert aber diese Nächstenliebe? Was ist ihr letztes Ziel? Wohin steuert dieser fundamentale „Instinkt" der Nächstenliebe?

Wenn wir Blickrichtung und Denken auf unsere irdische Existenz begrenzt halten, dann wird es uns wohl schwer werden, eine befriedigende Rechtfertigung für alle Mühen und Sorgen der Nächstenliebe zu finden. Sie ist eingeschrieben in uns, sagt man, genügt das aber, unser Opfer zu rechtfertigen? Sie trägt dazu bei, sagt man, Ordnung und Harmonie in der Gesellschaft zu gewährleisten. Ist das ein genügend starkes Motiv, auf unseren „natürlichen" Egoismus zu verzichten?

Nein. Die Nächstenliebe ist, ohne die höhere Seinsstufe einzubeziehen, nicht zu rechtfertigen. Nur von dieser anderen Dimension her erhält sie ihren Sinn. Dieses Höhere, dieses Jenseitige, dieses andere würden wir nur ahnen können, wenn Gott uns nicht tatsächlich seine Existenz offenbart hätte. Diese andere Dimension nennt sich das GOTTESREICH, und um Einlaß zu finden, ist die Nächstenliebe Voraussetzung.

Ist sie dann nichts weiter als ein Passierschein? Ist sie eine Prüfung, die, wenn wir sie bestehen, uns die Himmelstore öffnet? Ist sie das Lösegeld fürs ewige Reich oder ein Test für unseren guten Willen, mit dem wir uns dieses Glück verdienen, eingezahlt in einer Währung von 50 oder 60 Jahren Opferleben? ... Das ist doch vielfach die Meinung über den Begriff der Nächstenliebe, und es gibt genügend fromme Bücher dieser Sprache.

Nein. Die Nächstenliebe ist nichts von alledem! Sie hat ihren Wert in sich selbst, ihr Sinn liegt in ihrem Wesen begründet. Wenn die Nächstenliebe nur ein Test wäre, so könnte dieser Test auch auf irgendeinem andern Gebiet für uns erdacht und mit uns erprobt werden, und dieses „irgendein anderes" könnte dann keinerlei Beziehung haben zu einer erhofften Belohnung. Die Nächstenliebe hat im Gegensatz zu diesem Verdacht ihren Wert in sich selbst.

Durch die Nächstenliebe wird unsere Ewigkeit nicht verdient, sondern herangebildet und verwirklicht. Sie ist das Schußgarn, mit dem gewebt wird.

Der Himmel ist ja doch nichts anderes als die große Vereinigung der Menschen in der Einheit der Gottesliebe. Der Himmel ist ein großer Leib, der die Gesamtmenschheit organisch in sich vereint und miteinander eins werden läßt. Und das Leben, die Seele dieses Leibes, ist die Nächstenliebe. Sie ist nicht nur die Bedingung für den Himmel, sondern sie ist der Himmel selbst. Sie ist nicht nur der Weg zu einem zukünftigen Glück, sondern sie ist dieses Glück selbst, und dieses ist ewig, denn

die Liebe hört nimmer auf.

(I Korinther 13, 8a)

Die Liebe ist ewig, wie Gott selbst ewig ist. DEUS CARITAS EST.

Und hier sind wir am Ziel. Der Weg führte uns vom Egoismus, fest verwurzelt im Materiellen, bis zur vollkommen entfalteten Nächstenliebe im Seelischen und Geistigen.

Zwischen diesen beiden Polen spielten Sexualität und Mutterliebe bedeutsame Vermittlerrollen. Sie sind das verbindende Element, das diese Passage von einem zum andern ermöglicht hat. Diese Bewegung stellt die Spaltung einer Ur-Identität dar, die jedoch hinsichtlich einer definitiv transzendenten Einheit eine illusorische, aussichtslose Identität gewesen war. Doch es folgte der Schritt von dieser Identität zur wahren Einheit über die Nicht-Identität der Geschichte. Und die Nächstenliebe ist das, was der Geschichte erlaubt, ihren Kreislauf zu beenden. Denn seit Anbeginn verfolgt sie Schritt für Schritt ihr Ziel, bis zur wiedergefundenen wahren Einheit.

Worin diese Einheit genau bestehen wird, kann niemand von uns sagen, unser Vorstellungsvermögen reicht dafür nicht aus. Aber sie ist uns gewiß. Wir können behaupten, daß sich unsere gesamte Geschichte im Spannungszustand und im Lauf auf dieses Ziel hin befindet.

Originaltitel:
De l' identité de la matière à l' unité de la charité
(Beirut/Libanon 1961)

Die Krise in der Liebe und in der Freundschaft

Jede Liebe führt notwendigerweise in eine Krise. Indem sie der Flug ins Unendliche ist, erscheint mir mein Partner früher oder später in seiner Endlichkeit und Fragwürdigkeit. Er entweicht jetzt aus seinem Heiligenschein, mit dem ich ihn umgeben hatte, damals, während meiner Leidenschaft. Diese Entdeckung bringt mir plötzlich eine fortschreitende Enttäuschung. Das ist die Krise der Liebe. Und sie ist umso härter, schmerzvoller und anhaltender, je sinnlicher oder gefühlsverwirrender diese Liebe anfangs war.

Es ist sehr bedeutsam zu wissen, daß es diese Krise gibt und daß sie kommen wird, denn dann kann man sie mit Geduld und Klarsicht akzeptieren, wenn es soweit ist. Dann wird sie leichter überwunden werden, denn die Krise soll überwunden werden! Erst in der Überwindung erweist sich die Liebe als wahr und wird nun das Siegel der Treue erhalten. Keine Liebe ist je authentisch, wenn sie diese Krise nicht erlebt; und eine Liebe, die diese Krise nicht durchzustehen und zu meistern vermag, offenbart sich als unecht.

Worin besteht diese Krise nun wirklich?

Sie besteht im fortschreitenden Entdecken der Schwächen des anderen, seiner Grenzen, seiner großen und kleinen Fehler, die er ständig neu begeht. Diese Erkenntnis bewirkt eine Entzauberung und Ernüchterung, und je idealisierter ich das Porträt dieses geliebten Gesichtes gemalt hatte, umso größer mag die Ernüchterung sein. In der Stunde, in der der Geliebte entthront wird und kein Gott mehr ist, sondern ein Mensch wie alle anderen, erscheint er plötzlich geringer als alle anderen, denn man kennt ihn besser. Alles sinkt und wendet sich, aus Leidenschaft wird Kälte. Der andere wird jetzt als Belästigung empfunden, seine Anwesenheit reizt, und es mag sogar bis zum Ekel reichen. So fällt der Mensch von einem Extrem ins andere.

Wie ist eine solche Umkehr der Gefühle möglich, ein solcher Sturz ins Nichts? Der Grund ist der, daß das ganze Drama seit dem ersten Tag auf der Bühne der Emotion gespielt wird. Um aber den Zustand der inneren Freiheit im Liebeserlebnis zu erreichen und zu wahren, sollte man versuchen, die Ebene der Emotionen zu überschreiten, insbesondere die der sinnlichen Gefühlsverstrickungen.

Wie bewältigt man diese Krise?

Durch persönliche Anstrengung und festen Willen! Ich bewältige die Krise durch mein ernstes Bemühen, den tiefer liegenden Wert des anderen jenseits von all dem zu finden, an dem ich heute Anstoß nehme und das mich enttäuscht. Jetzt forsche ich bewußt nach seinen „guten Seiten", den allein wesentlichen, und diese liegen in ganz anderen Bereichen als äußerer Faszination, bestimmter Charakterzüge und persönlichem Charme, das mich in seiner Gesamtheit anfangs so gefangennahm und fesselte. Erst jetzt werde ich den anderen langsam immer besser und immer vollkommener sehen lernen. Ich will es, und daher versuche ich es. Ich arbeite daran, und daher wird es mir gelingen. Ich werde bis in seinen Wesensgrund vordringen und ihn ganz lieben – so wie er ist.

Möglicherweise wird hier ein blinder Glaubensakt notwendig, denn wenn ich mich dem wahren Wert des anderen nähern will, so setze ich diesen glaubend voraus. Später, nachdem ich diesen Glaubensakt vollzogen habe, forsche ich mit Geduld und Scharfsinn, bis die Liebe in mein Herz zurückkehrt. Die Wiederbegegnung mit dem anderen wird stattfinden, und zwar auf einer weit tieferen menschlicheren Ebene als zuvor.

Eine Liebeskrise kann als eine Chance zur viel persönlicheren Entdeckung des anderen verstanden werden und demnach als eine Neuentdeckung. Diesmal nicht in seinem Haben, sondern in seinem Sein. Diese Entdeckung ist wesentlich ernster als die erste, denn sie erfordert ein lang anhaltendes Bemühen um den anderen und gute Ausdauer meinerseits. Sie ist demnach eine Eroberung des anderen durch eigenes Opfer und gute Selbstüberwindung. Aber nur dieser selbstgewählte Prozeß bestätigt, daß man ernsthaft zu lieben imstande ist und den anderen zu lieben bereit ist, so wie er ist. Dann liebt man ihn nicht nur zur eigenen, wenn auch hohen Freude, nicht aus Eitelkeit, nicht um gewisser Vorteile willen, sondern ihn selbst und ihn allein.

Eine solche herangereifte Liebe wird wahrscheinlich nicht den idealistischen Traum erfüllen, dem man sich zu Beginn selig hingegeben hatte. Aber eine solche Liebe ist wahrer und stabiler, denn sie gründet jetzt in der Freiheit und wurzelt in der Person. Das letzte Stadium einer wahren Liebe ist die Treue. So gibt es drei Stadien im Liebesprozeß:

1. Leidenschaft und Verzauberung
2. Enttäuschung und Zweifel
3. Wahre Erkenntnis und Treue

Nur diese Art von Liebe, die gewillt ist, auch das dritte Stadium zu verwirklichen, ist würdig, den Namen „Liebe" zu führen.

Was für die Liebe gilt, gilt auch für die Freundschaft. Doch liegen die Höhepunkte im Freundschaftserlebnis nicht auf diesen Höhen, und die Tiefpunkte sind kein solches Drama. Die Krise ist weniger offensichtlich und weniger schmerzvoll als beim Liebeserlebnis. Dafür gibt es zwei Gründe: Zunächst ist es die Leidenschaft, die eine viel geringere Rolle in der Beziehung zwischen zwei Freunden spielt, denn das Verhalten zueinander ist von mehr Ruhe und Klarheit getragen. Das ist ein glücklicher Umstand, denn er verringert das Ausmaß der kritischen Phase, die auch hier folgt. Doch wird die Krise weniger scharf empfunden und weniger bewußt erfahren, sie mag sogar unbemerkt vorübergehen. In einem solchen Fall wächst aber die Freundschaft dennoch durch die schwelende Krise und wird durch das reine Gefühl füreinander in Treue gewandelt.

Diese Beschreibung einer geglückten Freundschaft könnte auch für die Liebe gelten, wenn diese ruhig, klar und vernünftig ist vom ersten Tag an. Die praktische Erfahrung lehrt uns, daß Ehen auf dieser Ausgangsbasis bessere Aussichten haben, sie sind stabiler und glücklicher.

Der zweite Grund, weshalb eine Freundschaftskrise weniger heftig und weniger schmerzvoll in Erscheinung tritt, ist in der Kontaktweise der Partner zu finden. Freunde verkehren weniger oft und weniger intim miteinander als Liebende. Die relative Unregelmäßigkeit, in der sich Freunde miteinander verabreden und sich mehr oder weniger, den äußeren Umständen entsprechend, wiedersehen, machen diese Beziehungen angenehm, interessant und wünschenswert. Aber auch zuviel intime Vertrautheit und überschwenglicher Eifer in der Freundschaft ist oft ein Grund zur Abkühlung. Wird sie dennoch beharrlich fortgesetzt, dann ermattet die Beziehung, und leider kommt es vor, daß eine „große Freundschaft" dann erlischt. Ein weises Sprichwort sagt daher:

Gute Zäune schaffen gute Nachbarn.

Original:
La crise de l' amour et de l' amité
(Chigaco/USA 1966)

Ein neues Integrationsvermögen kündigt sich an

Jede Hauptphase der Evolution wird im Bereich der Kreaturen von einer jeweils neuen Fähigkeit gekennzeichnet, die Außenwelt in sich aufzunehmen und doch deren Fortleben zu gewährleisten.

Auf biologischer Ebene besitzt das Auge ein Höchstmaß von Sinneseigenschaft und Perfektion in der Assimilierung des Wahrnehmbaren durch ein Integrationsvermögen, das die Objekte unbeschadet läßt. Als extremes Gegenbeispiel ist die Nahrungs- und Verdauungsfunktion zu nennen, die das Aufgenommene zerstört.

Auf der geistigen Ebene bietet der Gedanke eine neue Möglichkeit und öffnet dem Phänomen der Objekt-erhaltenden Integration eine neue Dimension. „Etwas denken" bedeutet, den Extrakt des erdachten Objektes in mir zu verinnerlichen, d. h. in mein Inneres einzulassen, indem ich es zugleich unabhängig von mir fortleben lasse. Der Gedanke entspricht auf der Ebene der Form dem des Auges auf der Ebene der Materie. Denken und Sehen.

Die Übereinstimmung dieser beiden Funktionen ist erstaunlich, denn beide haben als gemeinsamen Nenner und als gemeinsame Charakteristik den Vorteil, den vollkommenen Respekt mit der vollkommenen Einverleibung zu vereinen und miteinander zu versöhnen. Diese Analogie findet in der Umgangssprache ihren Ausdruck bei der Anwendung des Verbes „sehen", „einsehen", „verstehen". Im Englischen ist die Wendung „I see" im ständigen Gebrauch: „Ich sehe, was Sie sagen wollen" meint „ich verstehe". Im Französischen wird das „Sehen" für die Gotteserkenntnis genommen: „voir Dieu".

Die dritte Ebene betrifft die innere Person und gehört noch der Zukunft an. Diese wird in einem neuen Integrationsvermögen bestehen, die dem Menschen die innige Verschmelzung mit dem anderen auf intimste und vollkommenste Weise ermöglicht, doch ohne gegenseitige Unterwerfung, ohne das Dominieren des einen über den anderen. Diese Etappe wird die Zeit der voll ausgereiften Liebe werden, die es gelernt hat, Besitzstreben und Respekt miteinander zu versöhnen. Diese qualitativ neue Liebe bedeutet tiefes Einswerden der Partner – zugleich aber Distanz und klare Unterscheidung; sie bedeutet das Aufgehen im echten Gemeinsamen – zugleich aber gegenseitige Wahrung der Person. Diese Form der Liebe, diese Liebesweisheit, wird endlich den höchsten Traum des menschlichen Herzens verwirklichen.

Wir sind bereits in diese neue Phase der Entwicklung eingetreten, stehen jedoch noch ganz am Anfang, und unsere Idee über diese kommende Etappe ist noch vage. Vor uns weitet sich ein ganz neuer Weg voller Hoffnungen und voller Zusagen.

Die Vergangenheit ist der Garant für die Zukunft. Die anfänglich resistente Dichte der ersten Lebewesen gegen alle Außeneinflüsse entwickelte sich langsam fortschreitend zur Ausbildung von Wahrnehmungsorganen oder Sinnesorganen für den Austausch mit der Umwelt. Auch beim Menschen beobachten wir diese „Umstellung": Die beharrlichen, sturen Versuche des rein materiellen und noch dem Tier verwandten Besitzinstinktes des heranwachsenden Kleinkindes reifen langsam aus und wandeln sich zur Fähigkeit, die Dinge und Wesen seiner Umgebung durch ein Gedankengeflecht zu umschließen, um sie auf neue und ganz andere Weise zu besitzen.

So können wir sicher sein, daß die enttäuschenden Versuche der menschlichen Liebe, sich gegenseitig in sich hineinzunehmen, um sich beieinander und ineinander einzuschmelzen und ganz zu besitzen, eines Tages doch gelingen werden. Im Herzen von Mann und Frau lebt und schmerzt seit allen Zeiten dieses Verlangen und sehnt eine Lösung herbei. Eines Tages wird sich durch ein neues Integrationsvermögen die wahre Liebe verwirklichen, und die vollkommene Vereinigung wird möglich werden – jenseits aller Erwartung! ...

Original:
Vers une nouvelle faculté d' intégration
(Chigaco/USA 1966)

Ich vergebe dir

Die Fähigkeit des Vergebens stammt aus Gott. Derjenige unter uns, der vergeben kann, ist gottähnlich. *„Seid barmherzig wie euer Vater barmherzig ist ... Seid vollkommen, wie euer Vater vollkommen ist"* (Bergpredigt).

Vergeben heißt sein Herz ausdehnen, weit über das Maß des Vergebens des anderen hinaus soll es wachsen. Vergeben heißt, die Sünde des anderen auf sich ableiten und sie tief hineinnehmen in den Liebesgrund des eigenen Wesens. Dieser heimliche Anruf, dem anderen zu vergeben, ist zugleich eine Einladung, selbst über sich hinauszuwachsen und sich dabei zu vergessen. Demnach dient es beiden Seiten.

Dieses Wort oder diese Geste „Ich vergebe Dir" ist freilich außerordentlich schwer, denn es trifft den empfindlichsten Nerv des Menschen: unsere persönliche Würde, unsere menschliche Ehre, unser Selbstwertgefühl, und deshalb ist der Vollzug jedes wahren Vergebens ein heroischer Akt. Dem gläubigen Menschen fällt es ja doch tausendmal leichter, regelmäßig die Messe zu besuchen, fleißig zu beten und zu fasten, als seinem Mitmenschen zu vergeben.

In der Bergpredigt wird das Vergeben als eine Vorbedingung für das Fasten genannt. Zuerst spricht Jesus vom Vergeben:

Wenn ihr den Menschen ihre Fehler vergebt,
so wird euer himmlischer Vater auch euch vergeben.
Vergebet aber ihr den Menschen ihre Fehler nicht,
so wird euch euer Vater eure Fehler nicht vergeben.

Und wenn ihr Fasten haltet, so dürft ihr nicht
trübselig erscheinen wie die Heuchler. Sie entstellen
nämlich ihr Angesicht, damit die Menschen
sehen, daß sie fasten. Wahrlich, Ich sage euch,
sie haben ihren Lohn schon empfangen ...

(Matthäus 6, 14-18)

Wie oft gelten doch dem Menschen sein Fasten und Beten als ein „Alibi", um sich damit vom Akt seiner Vergebung selbst loszusprechen! Hier liegt eine der Gefahren des religiösen Kultus und der religiösen Praktiken im allgemeinen, die angeblich den Gläubigen von dem zweifellos unangenehmen Schritt seiner Vergebung befreien. Weitere Jesusworte aus der Bergpredigt:

Ich aber sage euch:
Wer seinem Bruder zürnt, wird dem Gerichte verfallen ...
Wenn du zum Beispiel deine Gabe zum Altar bringst
und dort fällt es dir ein, daß dein Bruder etwas
gegen dich habe, dann laß deine Gabe dort vor dem
Altar liegen, geh hin, versöhne dich zuvor mit deinem
Bruder, und dann erst magst du deine Gabe opfern.
Sei bereit, dich schnell mit deinem Gegner zu versöhnen,
solange du mit ihm noch auf dem Wege bist,
es könnte sonst dein Gegner dich dem Richter übergeben.

(Matthäus 5, aus 22-25)

Jahr für Jahr, wenn die Fastenzeit beginnt, erinnert uns die Kirche daran, damit wir dieser subtilen Illusion nicht verfallen, alles sei mit uns in Ordnung. Das notwendige „Ich vergebe dir" und unsere barmherzigen Werke bekommen ihren Stellenwert vor dem Fasten, vor dem Beten und vor allen anderen religiösen Praktiken. „Ich vergebe dir" – das bedeutet, dem anderen eine neue Chance geben, so wie auch Gott sie uns gewährt. „Siebenundsiebzigmal sieben mal" sollen wir dem anderen vergeben, nicht nur schwerfällig ein einziges Mal, heißt es an einer anderen Stelle des Evangeliums. Es bedeutet, den anderen ganz loszubinden und freizumachen, ihn neu aus sich heraustreten zu lassen, ihn herauszuführen aus seiner Sackgasse und ihm behilflich zu sein beim Finden eines neuen Anfangs. Es bedeutet, ihm Zuversicht zu geben, Glaube an die Tilgung einer Schuld. „Ich vergebe dir" – das bedeutet Erlösung, denn es will sagen: „Ich glaube an Dich!"

Und was uns, die Vergebenden betrifft, so führt uns dieser Akt unserer inneren Freiheit entgegen. Wir vergeben – und damit geben wir uns größer als das Böse, wir zeigen uns stärker als der Haß, unsere Liebe reicht tiefer als die Sünde. Haß und Groll hingegen erzeugen ein böses Gift in uns, das unser Blut und unseren Geist verderben kann, da Frieden und Freude uns verlassen. Die Verweigerung der Vergebung zerstört uns selbst ebenso wie den anderen, der ihrer bedarf, und darüber hinaus zerstört sie die Gemeinschaft, in der wir leben. „Ich vergebe dir", dieses Wort, diese Geste bedeutet den besten Sieg über uns selbst.

Original:
Pardon
(Kairo 1987)

Lebenszwänge und persönliche Freiheit

Die Zelle liegt am Ursprung meiner Existenz, mit ihr beginnt mein Werden. In dieser Zelle ist in Miniaturschrift die gesamte Geschichte der Menschheit und des Lebens seit ihrem Anfang festgehalten. Dieser winzige Lebenskeim verdichtet demnach die Vergangenheit dieser Erde in seinem Innern und zugleich enthält er mein individuelles Wesen, er enthält mein Lebensprogramm; dieses Programm wird sich nach langsamer Entfaltung eines Tages klar erkennen lassen. Meine persönliche Geschichte ist demnach eingeschrieben in diese erste Zelle.

Mein Leben ist jedoch nicht nur ein Aufblättern dieser Erbschaft, die mir durch einen Organismus gegeben wurde, denn dieser Organismus tritt ja bereits während der ersten Augenblicke seiner Existenz in Beziehung zur Umwelt. Erst aus dieser Wechselbeziehung resultiert die ganz bestimmte Art meines Wesens – und das bin ich.

Doch nun frage ich mich: Bin ich tatsächlich nichts anderes als nur das Produkt einer Wechselbeziehung zwischen einem gegebenen Organismus und dessen Umwelt? Gibt es keinen dritten Faktor, der hier hinzutritt, um diesen biologischen und gesellschaftlichen Determinismus in eine bestimmte Richtung zu lenken, wodurch ein Existenzsinn zu erkennen wäre? Diesen dritten Faktor gibt es – man nennt ihn FREIHEIT.

Macht man sich aber nicht lächerlich, wenn man heute im Kontext moderner Forschungsergebnisse auf den Gebieten von Biologie und Soziologie über die persönliche Freiheit spricht? Gibt es sie überhaupt? Gibt es einen einzigen Raum in dieser Welt, ein einziges Feld, auf dem ungehindert freie Aktivitäten entfaltet werden können? Oder bin ich unabänderlich festgelegt und festgehalten durch ein inneres und äußeres Kräftespiel, das mich knebelt, fesselt, knetet und nach fremden Wünschen formen will?

So scheint es, und doch kann eine wissenschaftliche Analyse vom Menschen nicht an der Freiheit vorbeigehen, sie kann sie nicht unerwähnt lassen, sie muß sie auf sachliche Art als Tatsache anführen, als eine zumindest unter anderen. Aber so wie der Chirurg in Zeit und Ewigkeit außerstande sein wird, mit dem Skalpell die Seele des Menschen zu finden, so werden auch die Soziologen niemals, auch nicht nach peinlichster Forschung, ihre Hand an etwas legen können, das man Freiheit nennt. So wie die Seele sich jeder objektiven Analyse des Reellen entzieht, so entzieht sich auch die Freiheit einer solchen Analyse. Die Freiheit gehört einer anderen Ordnung an, sie lebt in einer ganz anderen Dimension des Seins, und sie lebt überhaupt nur im Augenblick, in dem sie sich manifestiert.

Die Freiheit ist ein inneres Erlebnis und kein äußeres Studienobjekt. Die Freiheit ist Frucht einer menschlichen Erfahrung und nicht das Resultat einer intellektuellen Suche. Die Freiheit läßt sich eher spontan erfühlen und erkennen als sachlich und langwierig verifizieren, um sie verstandesmäßig erfassen zu können.

Keineswegs steht die Freiheit in Opposition zum Determinismus, d. h. zu allen Sorten von Vorbestimmungen und Lebenszwängen, sondern sie ist diesen allen übergeordnet. Freiheit und Determinismus erscheinen also nicht nebeneinander auf einer Ebene, sondern die Freiheit fügt sich ein in den Determinismus, sie kooperiert mit ihm, um ihm von innen her eine persönliche Richtung zu geben, d. h. ihn zu orientieren.

Reine Freiheit gibt es nicht. Jede Freiheit ist bedingt durch etwas anderes, und sie sucht sich inmitten mannigfacher Lebenszwänge selbst in ihrem Wesen. Diese Zwänge zu erkennen und sie anzunehmen, um sie aber bewußt als „arbeitenden Diener" für das persönliche Ziel einzusetzen, das ist das Geheimnis wahrer Freiheit.

Vorbestimmungen und Lebenszwänge sind Kräfte, die den Menschen fesseln und erdrücken können, oder sie sind ihm dienend behilflich zu seinem Besten. Alle Lebenskunst des Menschen besteht in der weisen Nutzanwendung dieser ihn angeblich behindernden Kräfte, sodaß man sie eines Tages dirigiert, anstatt sich von ihnen dirigieren und drangsalieren zu lassen. Wer mit seinem Determinismus „spielt", ihn sich geschmeidig und fügsam macht zum eigenen Gebrauch, der führt kluge Strategie und eine Lebenspolitik großer Weite.

Denn seinen Determinismus zu verleugnen, bedeutet nichts als Selbstbetrug, und gegen ihn ankämpfen bedeutet Energieverschleiß, denn es führt zu nichts. Das einzig sinnvolle Verhalten besteht in der Erkenntnis und Annahme der eigenen Grenzen und Beschränkungen. Diese voll zu akzeptieren und sie bewußt zu orientieren, das ist die einzig realistische Lösung des Problems.

Hat der Mensch nicht seit Beginn seiner Geschichte mit den Naturgewalten den Kampf aufgenommen, um sie für sich zu gewinnen? Was ist ein Windsegel und wozu dient es? Hat der Mensch nicht mit Regen und Feuer experimentiert? Was ist eine Kornmühle am reißenden Strom? Hat er nicht Energie gewonnen aus Wasser, Wind und Sonnenglut und ist bis zur Atomenergie vorgedrungen? Keinesfalls versuchte der Mensch, sinnlos gegen diese Energien von Natur und Kosmos anzurennen, um sie wie ein Drachentöter zu bezwingen, sondern im Gegenteil, Schritt für Schritt hat er sie gezähmt, gemeistert und sie sich dienstbar gemacht. Am Kampf mit der Natur und nicht gegen sie ist der Fortschritt des Menschen abzulesen. Gefürchtete Naturphänomene, die absolute Todesquellen für den Menschen dargestellt hatten, wurden von ihm in gute und nützliche Quellen „umfunktioniert".

So ist es mit der Freiheit bestellt. Allein das systematische Gefügigmachen seiner naturgegebenen Vorbestimmungen oder anderen Determinismen führt den Menschen langsam, aber sicher aus den Zwängen in die Freiheit. Die Freiheit ist ein „Arbeitsprojekt" an der eigenen Person und kein Geschenk. Sie ist mehr das Ziel als der Ausgangspunkt einer Bewegung. Der Mensch ist nicht frei geboren, sondern er wird frei. Oder sagen wir: Der Mensch erhebt sich schrittweise von der Ebene einer bislang nur möglichen oder zaghaft keimenden Freiheit auf die Ebene realer und wirksamer Freiheit. Dieser Aufstieg vollzieht sich beim Menschen in der fortschreitenden Meisterschaft seines Determinismus, der jetzt zum Spezialinstrument seiner Selbstverwirklichung geworden ist, zum Mittel seiner Selbstbesiegung. Dann ist er frei.

Das Programm des Embryos wie das Programm des gesellschaftlichen Rahmens, in dem ich heranwachse und mich entwickle, enthält für mich einen genügend großen Spielraum von Möglichkeiten, in dem ich fortwährend wählen kann und wählen soll. Diese Wahl hat mit dem Zufall nichts gemein, sondern sie vollzieht sich unter dem Zeichen meiner Vorbestimmungen und Zwänge. Sie beherrschen mich nicht, denn jetzt wird das Beste aus ihnen gemacht, und ich beherrsche sie.

Die Versuchung des heutigen Menschen ist stets dieselbe: Er deutet seinen Determinismus als schicksalgegeben, also als unabänderliche Vorbestimmung. Das Wort „Determinismus" meint die eindeutige Bestimmtheit allen Geschehens, insbesondere unseres Wollens und Handelns, durch eine Folge gegebener Ursachen. Und da der Mensch seine Vorbestimmungen als schicksalgegeben ansieht, bleibt er für ihn der ewige Vorwand, seine wichtige eigene Wahl zu umgehen. Ständig sind die meisten Menschen darauf fixiert, ihrem biologischen und gesellschaftlichen Determinismus viel zuviel Wert beizumessen, um damit der Verpflichtung zu entgehen, ihrem Leben durch einen tüchtigen Griff ins Räderwerk die eigene Note zu geben. Lieber flüchten sie sich hinter das Schutzschild eines angeblich in ihren Zellen oder irgendwo im Himmel vorgezeichneten Weges und hoffen, sich damit von ihrer Aufgabe, ihre Existenz allein aufzubauen – trotzdem! – dispensieren zu können.

Die Freiheit ist freilich eine Bürde. Sie hat ihr Gewicht. Im bequem gewordenen Menschen lebt deshalb das Unbehagen, die Angst vor der Freiheit, und er versucht, ihr zu entkommen. Tausende Gründe erfindet er, vor seiner entscheidenden Lebenswahl davonzulaufen. Dabei geht er von der theoretischen zur praktischen Verneinung der Freiheit über, indem er dieses kostbare Gut allen möglichen Molochen der gegenwärtigen Zivilisation zu Füßen legt, gerade so, wie er es in alten Zeiten tat, indem er seine Freiheit auf die Stufen der Synagoge oder der Kirche legte. Diese Flucht ist selten so gut beschrieben und erklärt worden wie in dem Buch von Erich Fromm „Die Flucht vor der Freiheit".

Inzwischen ist jedoch die Freiheit mehr denn je zu einer Herausforderung für den heutigen Menschen geworden. Die Zukunft unserer Welt wird wesentlich von der Haltung, die wir dem Freiheitsbegriff gegenüber einnehmen, geprägt werden, vor allem aber vom Wagnis unserer tatsächlichen Entscheidungen.

Original:
Liberté et déterminisme
(Kairo/Ägypten 1971)

Freiheit und Gnade

Meine innere Freiheit und mein tiefes Wollen sind mit der göttlichen Freiheit und dem göttlichen Willen identisch, es besteht Koinzidenz, d. h. beides fällt zusammen. Ich heiße den Willen Gottes gut und willige meinerseits ein, desgleichen nimmt Gott meine freie Wahl an, zu der mich sein Geist inspiriert hatte. Indem ich also tief innerlich mein eigenes Wesen annehme, nehme ich den Willen Gottes an und „unterzeichne" ihn, der ja das Tiefste ist, das in mir lebt und wirkt. Zwischen meinem innersten Selbst und Gott besteht kein Gegensatz, sondern Übereinstimmung.

Der göttliche Wille ist nicht irgendwo in ferne Himmelsräume eingeschrieben, sondern ins Herz meiner Freiheit wesenhaft als Inspiration. Daher ist meine bewußt-persönliche Wesensgestaltung und „den Willen Gottes tun" ein und dasselbe Tun. Menschliches Handeln ist die Synthese aus Menschlichem und Göttlichem. Es entfließt vollständig dem Menschen und vollständig Gott, es ist ganz Freiheit und ganz Gnade und besteht in der unauflöslichen Einheit dieser beiden. Die göttliche Gnade im Zentrum eines menschlichen Handlungsaktes vernichtet keineswegs unsere Freiheit oder schränkt sie ein, sondern sie fördert und verwirklicht unsere Freiheit. Menschliches Handeln bedeutet daher den Einklang von Freiheit und Gnade, es ist deren Synthese.

Die vermutete Gegensätzlichkeit zwischen Freiheit und Gnade, Mensch und Gott, liegt an der irrtümlichen Niveaugleichheit der beiden. Man stellt sie als zwei Größen auf derselben Ebene einander gegenüber, sodaß sie einander ausschließen müssen. In Wahrheit befinden sie sich jedoch in vertikaler Beziehung zueinander, in einer komplementären Rangordnung der Harmonie. So wie der Vater und der Sohn innerhalb der Dreifaltigkeit trotz ihrer Vereinigung wohl voneinander unterschieden sind, so sind auch Freiheit und Gnade im menschlichen Handlungsakt vereint anwesend und doch unterschieden voneinander. So wie der Geist untrennbar dem Vater und dem Sohn entströmt, so entströmt das freie Tun des Menschen untrennbar beiden – der Freiheit und der Gnade.

Je freier mein Wirken sich gestaltet, umso deutlicher tritt Gott hinzu, und je stärker Gott in mir am Wirken ist, umso freier werde ich dabei. Freiheit und Gnade stehen im direkten Verhältnis zueinander und nicht im umgekehrten, wie das bei zwei Dingen derselben Natur oder derselben Ordnung der Fall ist. Bestünde zwischen Freiheit und Gnade nur eine äußere Wechselbeziehung, dann käme es zur Opposition und letztlich zur gegenseitigen Tilgung. Es handelt sich jedoch um eine tief innerliche und einander ergänzende Beziehung im gegenseitigen Durchdringen.

Nein, der Wille Gottes, den ich in mir spüre, ist kein bereits vorgezeichneter Plan, den ich auszuführen habe, sondern ein unmerkliches zartes Anrühren, ein geheimer Impuls, der mich auf meiner eigenen Linie in Bewegung setzt, ganz meiner Natur entsprechend und meinem Ziel der eigenen Verwirklichung entgegen. Demnach bedeutet für mich „den Willen Gottes tun" meine Selbstverwirklichung, meine Vollendung im tief Persönlichen.

Indem Christus nach dem Willen des Vaters handelte, kam er seiner innersten Berufung nach, welche darin bestand, wirklich voll und ganz Sohn zu sein. Der Wille des Vaters war in ihm keine Vergewaltigung seines eigenen Willens, sondern tiefster Ausdruck seines Wesens. Deshalb sagte er:

Es ist meine Nahrung, den Willen Gottes zu tun,
(Johannes 4, 31)

denn so wie die Nahrung vom Organismus assimiliert wird, um mit ihm eins zu werden, so wurde der Wille Gottes in Jesus zum integrierenden Bestandteil seines persönlichsten Wesens. So wie die Nahrung für den Körper nicht Kräfteschwund und Rückbildung bedeutet, sondern Wachstum und Gedeihen, so bedeutet für Jesus die Befolgung des göttlichen Willens nicht Last und Verfremdung, sondern das Mittel, um sein Wesen als Sohn voll zur Entfaltung zu bringen.

Und so steht es mit dem Menschen. Denn Christus ist das Muster für jedes Menschenwesen, er ist daher der vollkommene Mensch, weil er in ganzer Abhängigkeit vom Vater lebt. Die Vollkommenheit seiner menschlichen Natur ist die logische Konsequenz seiner bedingungslosen Unterwerfung unter den Vater.

Er war vollkommen geworden durch seinen Gehorsam.
(Hebräerbrief 5, 8)

Gerade jenes also, was den Menschen zu mindern scheint, das wird ihn fördern und erhöhen.

Solange Gott jedoch als der große Fremde verstanden wird, das ferne, hoch über uns erhabene und unerreichbere Wesen, solange wird sein Handeln als Macht über den Menschen empfunden, und durch sein Eingreifen geschieht Entfremdung. Wird Gott aber als vertrauter Gast, anwesend in der menschlichen Seele, erfahren, der uns näher ist, als wir uns selbst nahe sind, dann geschieht das Gegenteil – wahrer Austausch und beiderseitiges Durchdringen.

Gott hat es auf den Menschen abgesehen! Und auf unsere Welt! Doch ist dieses Verlangen keine fest fixierte Planung, denn die Liebe ist im Spiel! Gott folgt einer spontanen Herzensregung, es ist die Inspiration der Liebe, die hier Richtung weist im Sinne von „mehr" und „besser". Diese Inspiration und diese Orientierung, die sie gibt, sind in der Lage, tausend Formen und tausend Gesichter anzunehmen, ganz nach der Wahl des einzelnen Menschen, vollzogen nach seinem freien Willen. Daher ist menschliches Handeln tatsächlich freie Schöpfung und keine sklavische Befolgung von Geboten oder die Ausführung abgesteckter Gottespläne. Zwischen Gott und dem Menschen besteht weder Gleichnamigkeit noch Doppelsinnigkeit, sondern Analogie, d. h. eine übereinstimmende Ähnlichkeit. Weil beide nicht auf derselben Ebene stehen, kann es auch zu keinem Konflikt kommen, es gibt kein gegenseitiges Ausschließen, sondern ganz im Gegenteil: innere Ergänzung.

Meine menschliche Natur ist bereits in ihrer Eigenart ein „Anruf Gottes" und daher meine Berufung. Folge ich meiner Natur, dann folge ich dem Gottesruf in mir und erfülle damit meine Berufung. Etwas wollen, was ich zutiefst wünsche, heißt den Willen Gottes im Herzen vernehmen.

Original:
Liberté et Grâce
(Kairo/Ägypten 1981)

Der Tod als Wiedereinsetzung
und
Rückkehr zur Erde

Der Tod ist der Moment, in dem jeder von uns in den großen Lebensstrom zurückfließt, aus dem er hervorgegangen war. Diese Wiedereinsetzung

ist nicht Auflösung im Anonymen,
sondern Steigerung im Persönlichen;

ist nicht Rückkehr zur Ur-Energie,
sondern Selbstüberschreitung in der Liebe;

ist nicht Rücklauf ins Zeitlose,
sondern Eintritt ins Ewige;

ist nicht Aufzehrung,
sondern Aufstieg;

ist nicht Versinken im Unbewußten,
sondern Ekstase im Überbewußten;

ist nicht Zerstörung,
sondern V e r w i r k l i c h u n g.

Die Toten beginnen dann zu wirken. Sie fügen sich den Lebenden bei und führen ihnen zusätzliches Leben zu. Die Toten ziehen sich nicht in einen außerirdischen Bereich des Universums zurück, um dort ein Leben unter ihresgleichen zu führen, sondern sie finden sich gerade durch den Akt ihres Sterbens wieder eingesetzt in den Lebensfluß, der sie hervorgebracht hatte.

Die Toten erleben jetzt eine Verstärkung ihrer Gegenwart. Ihr Tod führt sie nicht fort von uns, sondern in unsere intime Nähe, und diese Nähe ist ein Vielfaches definitiver, als sie es je zuvor sein konnte. In ihrer Seelenkraft werden sie nun zu einem Ferment für uns Lebende. Durch die Gegenwart der Toten erhebt sich die menschliche Gemeinschaft langsam Schritt für Schritt und wird eines Tages ihre Vollendung finden. Die Toten sind der Antriebsmotor der Entwicklung und allen Fortschreitens. Durch sie bahnt sich die Evolution langsam ihren Weg zum Endziel.

Jeder von uns wird von der Gesamtlinie seiner Ahnen getragen, er versammelt in sich deren Leben; doch nicht deren Leben von einst, sondern ihre unsterbliche Existenz von damals und heute, denn hier handelt es sich nicht um eine symbolische, figurative Sprache, sondern um ein reelles, ontologisches Faktum – eine Tatsache. Alle Toten leben, sie leben wirklich, und sie leben fort in mir.

Wenn die Menschheit wächst und fortschreitet in ihrer Entwicklung, dann aufgrund der Gemeinschaft der Toten in ihrer Mitte, die immerzu aktiv sind und von innen ihren Druck auf unsere Welt ausüben. Die „andere Welt" ist innerhalb dieser Welt, das Jenseits ist hier.

Die frühere Menschheit addiert sich zur heutigen durch die fortwährende Wiedereinsetzung der Toten. Die gegenwärtige Menschheit ist nichts anderes als die Zusammenfassung der Gesamtmenschheit, die bereits gelebt hat. Wir tragen in uns diese tatsächliche, aber versteckte Gegenwart aller Menschen von einst. Diese Akkumulation ist es, die eine Evolution möglich macht. Es gibt nur Fortschritt dank dieses Zusammenschlusses – und dieser ist nur in und durch die überzeitliche Liebe möglich.

Die Liebe allein erlaubt der Menschheit nicht nur eine einfache Zusammenführung von Tod und Leben, sondern das wirkliche innere Zusammenwirken beider – in einem echten Bündnis.

Original:
La Mort comme reintégration et retour à la terre
(Chicago/USA 1967)

Vom Sinn der Erde

Plädoyer für eine Spiritualität der Inkarnation

Nachdem das WORT Fleisch geworden ist, nachdem das WORT Materie geworden ist, trägt nun alles Fleisch und alle Materie die Züge des inkarnierten WORTES und kündet von diesem Geheimnis.

Diesen Sichtwinkel einnehmen und alles in der Perspektive des Ereignisses der Inkarnation sehen bedeutet für uns das plötzliche Innewerden der Gottesgegenwart in der Mitte der Welt. Ohne dieses Wissen und diese Sicht fällt es nicht unbedingt leicht, Gottes lebendige und wirkende Anwesenheit wirklich zu erkennen. Paulus versuchte es den Athenern zu erklären, die noch nichts von der Inkarnation wußten. Als er zu ihnen von Gott sprach, den sie den „Unbekannten" nannten, sagte er:

Er selber spendet allem Leben, Odem und gar alles ...
Die Menschen sollten suchen, ob sie Ihn herausfühlten
und fänden, Ihn, der ja keinem aus uns ferne ist.
In Ihm leben wir, bewegen wir uns und sind wir.

(Apostelgeschichte 17)

Um diese göttliche Allgegenwart aber persönlich und tief innerlich zu erfahren, müssen wir uns ins Herz der Realität versenken, ins Herz der Natur. Es muß so tiefreichend geschehen, daß ich es zu Zeiten „religiöse Sinnlichkeit" nenne, wenn ich bei meinen Exerzitien eine bestimmte Haltung zeichnen will, die sich der Welt gegenüber offen und empfänglich zeigt. Diese Form einer Spiritualität steht derjenigen der strikten Weltentsagung gegenüber, die eine generelle Enthaltsamkeit proklamiert und dabei riskiert, den inneren Menschen gänzlich auszutrocknen. Sie will ihn hindern, sich diesen oder jenen irdischen Wirklichkeiten zu öffnen, die vielleicht Trägerinnen äußerst reicher und wichtiger Botschaften für ihn sein könnten.

Der spirituelle Mensch wird im allgemeinen dem sinnlichen Menschen gegenübergestellt, als ob ein geistig wachsendes und sich entfaltendes Wesen langsam, aber sicher seine sinnliche Wahrnehmung einbüßte, weil seine Sinne taub würden! Dieser Mensch wird dann, so glaubt man, nicht mehr fähig sein, irdische Lebensaspekte zu begreifen und mit allem Schönen, das die Welt uns bietet, mitzuschwingen. In der religiösen Geschichte wird uns aber das Gegenteil offenbart. Sie berichtet von den großen Mystikern in ihrer außerordentlich starken Gefühlskraft, um nicht zu sagen Sinnlichkeit. Das Mysterium des Schönen hat diese Menschen bis ins Innerste berührt, und indem sie das Erlebte in Worte fassen wollten, wurden aus ihnen Dichter und Künstler. Franz von Assisi und Johannes vom Kreuz waren Männer, zu denen die Erde sprach. Sie sprach zu ihnen eine geheimnisvoll-mystische, eine heilige, eine göttliche Sprache.

Es existiert jedoch ein spirituelles Schmalkostrezept der dauernden Entbehrungen, durch das wir nicht wachsen und mehr werden, sondern ärmer und weniger, denn es nimmt uns das Lebendige. Je mehr nämlich ein Mensch in die geistige Welt hineinreift, umso empfindsamer wird er gegenüber den irdischen und sinnlichen Dingen. Daher wurde in unserer Zeit eine Strömung geboren, die uns jenes ZURÜCK ZUR NATUR dringend ans Herz legt und lehrt, den SINN DER ERDE neu zu entdecken. Nietzsche hat es gepredigt, Victor Poucel und Teilhard de Chardin, Prediger der Neuzeit, jeder auf seine Art. Und sie brachten uns zurück zur Quelle des Christentums - zur INKARNATION.

Nietzsche hat uns vermutlich am schärfsten herausgefordert und uns Christen verpflichtet, erneut auf die Suche nach unserem Erbe zu gehen. Dort, von der wahren Quelle, sollen wir trinken! Dieser Prophet unserer Zeit stellte uns urplötzlich die Frage: Hat nicht das Christentum den Menschen ganz entmannt? Hat es ihm nicht alle Vitalität genommen, alle Frische, allen Lebensschwung? Hat es uns nicht in gewisser Hinsicht kastriert und uns den Geschmack am Leben genommen? ... Und auch ich frage mich: Hat sich das Christentum nicht zu einem verkappten Platonismus entwickelt, der uns einredet, uns in „reinen Ideen" zu ergehen, anstatt das zu sein, was es in Wahrheit ist, nämlich

EINE MYSTIK DER INKARNATION ...?

„Meine Brüder! Bleibt der Erde treu mit der ganzen Kraft Eurer Tugend!" Auf diese Weise provozierte uns Nietzsche eindringlich. Ja, diese Tugend, die Ihr in Euch tragt, veranlaßte Euch bisher, Euch von der Erde zu entfernen. Nutzt sie jetzt, um Euch mit derselben Entschiedenheit wieder an sie zu binden! Übertragen auf den individuellen Fall: Eine Ablösung, die zuvor keine Bindung gewesen ist, ist keine Ablösung, sondern pure Illusion, denn das Ergebnis kann kein Ergebnis sein, weil es aus dem Nichts kommt und ins Nichts führt. Wenn meiner Lossagung keine reale Bindung voranging, dann verliert der Akt meines „tapferen Verzichts" allen Wert und alle Bedeutung, weil es ja gar nichts gab, wovon ich mich gelöst haben könnte. So höre ich von Menschen, die tatsächlich glauben, von allem abgelöst zu sein, weil sie niemals in ihrem Leben geliebt haben. Diese Wesen sind mir keine Vorbilder, sondern arme Existenzen. Zunächst muß die Seele einmal aufgegangen sein in dieser Welt, man muß tief geatmet und die Dinge und Wesen geliebt haben, um später ohne Illusion und in ganzer Ehrlichkeit die Dimension der Überschreitung und Sublimierung leben zu können.

Jedes authentische spirituelle Leben läßt diesen dreifachen Schritt zu, den man in der scholastischen Fachsprache VIA AFFIRMATIVA – VIA NEGATIVA – VIA EMINENTALE nannte, oder, in anderen Worten:

ENGAGEMENT – AUFGABE – SUBLIMIERUNG
EINTAUCHEN – ABLÖSUNG – EKSTASE

Ohne den ersten Schritt, der uns befähigt, den Rhythmus der irdischen Wirklichkeit mitzuleben, indem unser Herz mit dem Herzen der Dinge und Wesen „mitklopft", kann vom zweiten Schritt keine Rede sein, sondern nur von einer innermenschlichen Verarmung. Hiergegen fühlte sich Nietzsche berufen anzugehen. Ich lese in seinem „Also sprach Zarathustra", Teil I, Kapitel „Von der schenkenden Tugend":

> Bleibt mir der Erde treu, meine Brüder, mit der Macht
> eurer Tugend! Eure schenkende Liebe und eure Erkenntnis
> diene dem Sinn der Erde! Also bitte und beschwöre ich
> euch: Laßt sie nicht davonfliegen vom Irdischen und mit
> den Flügeln gegen ewige Wände schlagen! Ach, es gab
> immer so viel verflogene Tugend!

(Nietzsche)

Weil der Baum sich tief im Erdreich eingewurzelt hat, deshalb kann er sich jetzt weit hinauf zum Himmel schwingen. Wenn die wahre Kontemplation als ein „geistiger Höhenflug" erlebt wird, dann deshalb, weil man mit beiden Füßen fest auf der Erde steht. Jedes Gebet, das nicht im echten Sinn in der Erde eingewurzelt ist wie ein Baum, läuft Gefahr, sich rasch zu verflüchtigen oder abzugleiten ins Abstrakte. Dem Baum ist sogar ein Verhältnismaß abzulesen: Je tiefer seine Wurzeln in die Erde reichen und je weiter sie sich dort verzweigen, umso höher ragen seine Zweige ins Licht. Je erdverbundener, umso näher dem Himmel. Das Geistige ist ja nicht der andere Pol des Körperlich-Materiellen und sein Opponent, sondern im Gegenteil, es ist seine Ergänzung, sein Kamerad. In dem Maß, in dem ich mir den Sinn für die Erde erwerbe, erwerbe ich mir auch den Sinn für den Himmel und umgekehrt.

Diese Wahrheit drückt die Bibel in überreicher Bildsymbolik aus. Auch die Liturgie unserer Messe vermittelt sie deutlich. Um aber den Sinn dieser Symbolsprache zu verstehen, und damit die Bilder unser Herz erreichen, muß uns der Hintergrund bekannt sein, auf den sie sich beziehen, d. h. die „leibhaftige" Wirklichkeit, die man an sich selbst erfahren haben sollte. Ein Symbol gibt nur demjenigen etwas, der die Sprache, die symbolisiert, kennt. Es darf keine Fremdsprache für ihn sein, und je tiefer sie ihm vertraut ist, umso näher rückt ihm der Symbolgehalt. Wenn wir also nicht selbst einmal in dieser Wirklichkeit gestanden und sie uns zu eigen gemacht hätten, dann bliebe uns ihr Symbol ein leeres Zeichen.

Sage ich „Wasser" zu jemandem, der noch niemals im brandenden Meer untertauchte oder der noch nie eine höllische Dursterfahrung hatte an einem Hundstag im Sommer, dem bleibt es ein leeres Wort. Auch den starken Sinn des Wortes „Licht" versteht man am besten, wenn man die nackte Sonne des Orients kennt, die, im Zenit stehend, alles ausbleicht und betäubt, wobei sie die farbige Natur in jenes seltsam flammende Weiß verwandelt. Damit wir den Sinn der Symbole entschlüsseln und ihre besondere Botschaft verstehen, die sie an uns richten, müssen wir von der Konsistenz, den Farben und dem Geschmack der Erde Wissen haben. Die geistige Wirklichkeit ist nicht etwas hoch Erhabenes über die physische, sondern sie ist in der physischen enthalten! Das Geistige ist im Materiellen und Leiblichen anwesend.

Desgleichen ist Gott nicht dieser kosmisch ferne Weltgeist, unbestimmbar jenseits alles Irdischen, und den zu erreichen wir uns erst mühsam aus dieser Welt herausheben und auf sie verzichten müssen, ihr entfliehen und allem entsagen müssen, sondern Gott ist in der Mitte dieser Welt zu finden, im Herzen des Seins, zu dem wir selbst gehören.

Wenn uns die Dinge heimlich auf ihre Transparenz hinweisen wollen, dann senden sie uns damit nicht fort in einen äußeren Wirklichkeitsbereich, sondern sie laden uns ein, in ihr Innerstes einzutreten und das Mysterium dort zu erspüren. Als ich in Alexandria einen Vortrag über die Bezüge zwischen Materie und Gebet gehalten habe – „Meine Gotteserfahrung im Zentrum der Materie" – brachte ich für die Anwesenden hübsche Steine vom Strand mit. Ich teilte sie aus und ließ sie während dieser Vortragszeit in den Händen halten. Mittels dieser Aktivierung unseres Tastsinnes, mittels des konkreten Kontaktes mit der Materie, mittels des feinsinnigen Empfindens der glattgewaschenen Oberfläche, der Rundungen, Beständigkeit, Schwere und Härte haben wir an diesem Abend zusammen Gottes Anwesenheit in der materiellen Welt „ertastet". Wir haben versucht, diese Dimension Gottes im doppelten Sinn zu „begreifen". Und wirklich, anhand dieser festen und dichten Weltrealität „Stein" haben wir etwas mehr über das Gottesmysterium erfahren können ...

Dieses Etwas mußte buchstäblich zuerst einmal materiell von uns „erfaßt" und „begriffen" werden, bevor wir die geistige Botschaft erfassen konnten. Diese war keineswegs dem materiellen Objekt fremd und mußte erst von ferne „herangedacht" werden, sondern sie entsprang aus ihrem Innern in unseren Händen. Deshalb ergänzte Nietzsche seinen Appell:

> Führt, gleich mir, die verflogene Tugend zur Erde
> zurück – ja, zurück zu Leib und Leben: daß sie der
> Erde ihren Sinn gebe, einen Menschen-Sinn!
>
> (Nietzsche)

Wenn wir nicht fähig werden, den Strom alles Lebendigen und Menschlichen aufzunehmen, wie könnten wir dann dem Leben seinen Sinn geben? Es geht ja nicht um den äußeren, sondern um den inneren Sinngehalt, den wir selbst entschlüsseln sollen. Wenn es uns nicht gelingt, diesen Sinn aus dem Herzen der Welt zu lesen, dann werden auch unsere Worte, die wir zu den Menschen sprechen, sinnlos sein. Nichts können wir ihnen dann geben als eine blutleere Rede ohne jede anwendbare Lebensbotschaft. Vor allem wir Geistlichen sollten uns nicht erlauben zu sagen: „Wir sind Geistliche, also bringen wir den Menschen den Sinn von oben."

Nein. Der Sinn findet sich im Objekt selbst, der Sinn liegt in der Erde selbst, dort hat Gott ihn hineingegeben und versteckt, so wie er die Mandel im Kern vor uns versteckte, damit wir sie finden sollen.

> Hundertfältig verflog und vergriff sich bisher
> so Geist wie Tugend. Ach, in unserm Leibe wohnt
> jetzt noch all dieser Wahn und Fehlgriff:
> Leib und Wille ist er da geworden. Hundertfältig
> versuchte und verirrte sich bisher so Geist wie
> Tugend. Ja, ein Versuch war der Mensch. Ach, viel
> Unwissen und Irrtum ist an uns Leib geworden! ...
> Euer Geist und eure Tugend diene dem Sinne der
> Erde, meine Brüder: und aller Dinge Wert werde
> neu von euch gesetzt!
>
> (Nietzsche)

Vielleicht sollten wir mehr auf die Dichter hören, um über die Poesie zur Mystik zu gelangen. Es gibt ein Buch mit dem Titel „Poesie und Mystik" von Henri Bremond, das nach dem Unterschied zwischen diesen beiden Begriffen forscht. Hat jede Dichtung etwas Mystisches? Ist sie Mystik? Und ist alle Mystik Dichtung? ... Tatsächlich vibrieren Herz und Sinne der beiden, des Dichters wie des Mystikers, angesichts der Natur und aller Schönheit dieser Welt. Was aber macht ihren Unterschied aus? Weshalb nennt man den einen Dichter und den anderen einen Mystiker?

Ich persönlich glaube, daß der Dichter vorzeitig haltmacht. Er bricht nicht durch bis zum Kern der Dinge, um die Mandel zu finden, das Letzte, das Kostbarste. Es geht ihm nicht wirklich auf, daß das Herz einer bestimmten Wirklichkeit, die er rühmt und großartig in seiner Kunst zu besingen weiß, Gott selbst ist. Doch nehmen sie beide denselben Anlauf, denn der Mystiker muß zunächst ein Dichter sein. Auch er muß die Fähigkeit zum heimlichen Gespräch mit der Natur besitzen, und schließlich muß er mit einem transparenten Blick gesegnet sein, der durchlässig ist für das innere Mysterium der

Erscheinung. Daher muß er über ein äußerst sensibles Gemüt verfügen, fast möchte ich sagen, er muß die Gabe der Verwundbarkeit haben, damit die Wesen ihn wirklich berühren und bis ins Innerste treffen können. Er muß eine sehr starke Erlebniskraft besitzen, die tief und intensiv zu fühlen vermag. Dieser Widerhall der Welt in einer mystisch befähigten Seele bedeutet die erste Etappe, die notwendig ist auf dem Wege zur Gotteserkenntnis in mystischer Schau.

In derselben Ideenfamilie siedle ich das folgende an: Ich meine, daß die NÄCHSTENLIEBE den EROS erfordert wie der Baum den Humus, in dem er steht. Gewöhnlich sagt man, daß die Agape jene edle Liebe sei, die vollkommen selbstlos zu geben weiß, und vom Eros behauptet man, er sei die Lust des egozentrischen Genießens. Ich glaube aber, daß wir eine solche Gegenübersetzung überwinden müssen. Man bemüht sich bereits darum, es gibt Bücher von dem Schweden Anders Nygren und von dem Franzosen Martin D' Arcy über das Thema von Eros und Agape.

Nach meinem Empfinden wurzelt alle Nächstenliebe im Eros. Es beginnt mit einem notwendigen „Lusthaben", dem anderen zu helfen, ihn lieben und betreuen zu wollen. Sehr gern will man es tun, man hat „Lust", sich zu geben. Später wird sich unsere Hinwendung dann entwickeln und zur wirksamen Nächstenliebe entfalten, doch anfangs verspüren wir nur diesen „Anreiz" zum Engagement; wir fühlen uns angezogen vom bedürftigen Nächsten, der uns „verführt", weil er uns braucht. Und das ist gut, sehr gut! Durch diese Wechselbeziehung bekommt unsere Nächstenliebe einen menschlichen Boden, auf dem allein sie gedeihen kann. Dann wird gewiß kein mechanischer Dienst verübt, der uns abgleiten könnte ins Abstrakte und damit Herzlose.

DIE WELT LIEBEN! ... Auch unser Gebet sollte sich gelegentlich von der Kunst und der Schönheit ernähren oder von guter Musik. Ein liebes Foto, ein schönes Musikstück, eine bestimmte Landschaft kann uns zur besten Gebetshilfe werden, und das hat die Kirche von jeher sehr gut verstanden. Sie benutzt in der feierlichen Liturgie unserer Messe alles, was das Gefühl tief anspricht und das Herz erhebt. Das geht einher mit der griechischen Bedeutung des sehr alten, antiken Wortes „Leiturgia", das „Dienst am Volk" bedeutet. Wir dürfen während der Meßliturgie, zumindest noch heute an den Hochfesten, alle fünf Sinne gebrauchen – ein „Dienst am Volk".

Die bildende Kunst, die Musik, die Schönheit der Natur und die Liturgie der Messe! Auch die Poesie versetzt uns in einen Gebetszustand. Menschen wie Claudel, Rimbaud, Baudelaire, Hugo, Verlaine – um nur einige französische Dichter zu nennen – waren leuchtende Sterne, die das Leben von Mensch und Welt in erschütternder Weise spiegelten. In solcher Wahrheit geschah es, daß ihre Verse ein Mittel wurden, um müde Herzen wieder in Gang zu setzen und einen Weg ins Innere der Erscheinungen zu weisen. Wenn unser spirituelles Leben zu welken droht, dann sollten wir uns, bevor es verkümmert, unbedingt fragen, ob es nicht Wasser braucht und ob wir ihm nicht zudem einen bestimmten Nährstoff vorenthalten.

Hat der hl. Ignatius nicht die „Anwendung der Sinne" als Gebetsmittel empfohlen und für den Beginn auch eine „Ortsbestimmung"? Dieser große Ordensmann, befähigt, streng und abstrakt zu denken, dem man einen stählernen Willen nachsagte, war zugleich mystisch genug, um uns aufzufordern, unsere Sinne zu aktivieren. Wir sollen uns üben im bewußten Sehen, bewußten Hören, bewußten Fühlen und Berühren. Eine biblische Szene sollen wir in sehr phantasievoller Weise innerlich ausschmückend betrachten, indem wir allerlei äußere Gegebenheiten dazuerfinden, um unser Erlebnisvermögen dieser entscheidenden Szene zu verstärken. Alles wurzelt im Gefühl, selbst die erhabenste Mystik kommt dorther. Das scholastische Sprichwort sagt:

Nichts ist im Kopf, das zuvor nicht in den Sinnen war.

Dieses Wort kann ohne weiteres auch für das Gebetsleben angewandt werden. Wohlverstanden heißt das nicht, daß wir uns dort für immer festsetzen sollten, um uns vornehmlich in rein ästhetischen Genüssen zu ergehen oder am Künstlerischen zu sättigen. Wer aber diesen Weg einschlägt und ihn konsequent durchläuft, dem wird Gott unterwegs mit Sicherheit begegnen! ... Ihm wird im Herzen der Weltrealität die göttliche Anwesenheit zum Erlebnis werden, denn Gott ist innerweltlich erfahrbar.

Mystik bedeutet nicht nur vereinfacht „Gemeinschaft mit der Welt", sondern sie ist Gemeinschaft mit Gott durch die Welt und mittels der Welt. Sie ist das behutsame Enthüllen eines Gesichtes und das Erkennen des Geliebten – jenseits alles Materiellen in seiner Dichte. Die Kunst, die Poesie, die Schönheit werden mir dann auf meinem Weg zu Ihm gedient haben. Deshalb glaube ich nicht, daß wir uns dies ersparen sollten, indem wir den Weg abkürzen. Da Gott sich überall in der Welt überreich verströmt und hindurchscheint durch die Dinge und Wesen, denke ich nicht, daß man ihn wirklich finden wird, wenn man auf den „Umweg" durch seine materielle Schöpfung verzichtet.

Ein großer Theoretiker moderner Kommunikationsmittel hat gesagt:

> Das Medium ist schon die Botschaft.
> Das Mittel, wodurch die Botschaft erbracht wird,
> ist die Botschaft selbst.
>
> (Marshall McLuhan)

In der erschaffenen Welt ist jede Erscheinung schon eine GOTTES-BOTSCHAFT. Lernen wir, diese zu lesen! Die Welt öffnet mir letztlich nur ihr göttliches Wesen im Maß meines geistigen Überschreitenwollens des Weltlichen. Überschreiten und sublimieren kann ich es jedoch nur, wenn ich mich zuvor darin versenkt hatte und es wirklich kenne.

Den Schlußgedanken überlasse ich Nietzsche:

> Tausend Pfade gibt es,
> die noch nie gegangen sind,
> tausend Gesundheiten und
> verborgene Eilande des Lebens.
> Unerschöpft und unentdeckt
> ist immer noch Mensch und Menschen-Erde ...
>
> Wahrlich, eine Stätte der Genesung
> soll noch die Erde werden!
> Und schon liegt ein neuer Geruch um sie,
> ein Heil bringender, und eine neue Hoffnung!

Dieser Appell zur Erdverbundenheit ist endlich gehört worden, und Nietzsche ist zum großen Teil daran beteilgt. Dieser Weg führte das Christentum glücklicherweise zu einer Neubesinnung auf seine Dimension der I n k a r n a t i o n.

Original:
Le sens de la Terre. Pour une spiritualité d' incarnation
(Kairo/Ägypten1986)

Von der Mystik der Natur

Plädoyer für eine Mystik der Inkarnation

Die Natur, uns allen wahrhaftig ein Mysterium, ist für uns gleichzeitig eine Einladung, ja eine Verlockung, dem Gottesmysterium näherzukommen. WER SICH DER NATUR HINGIBT, GIBT SICH GOTT HIN, heißt es aus menschlicher Erfahrung – denn wir empfinden die Erde in ihrer Reinheit, jung und unversehrt, als hätte sie die Hände ihres Schöpfers soeben verlassen. Ehrfürchtig stehen wir am Ursprung der Welt, an den Quellen des ersten Werdens, im Paradies ...

Ursprung der Rufe aus der Tiefe des Menschen,
scheinbar nur das Echo seiner Wünsche,
und doch fordert er mehr, als ihm möglich ist.
Wenn der Mensch ihm nahekommt, wird er wachsen.

Urgrund aller Eingebung in der Suche des Menschen,
scheinbar nur die Frucht seiner Arbeit,
und doch schenkt er ihm mehr, als er erwartet.
Erst wenn er aufscheint, wird der Mensch wirklich leben.

Geheime Wirklichkeit im Herzen der Existenz,
sie gibt ihr Sinn und fast ein Gesicht
in der Stunde des Lichts.
Ihr Verschwinden bedeutet Trennung
und Verlust allen Sinns.

Freiheit, Liebe, Geburt – ohne Anfang und ohne Ende,
wir sind durch Dich,
wir sind für Dich.
In uns zeugst Du Dich aus unserm Innern.

(Marcel Légaut)

Vermutlich haben Sie von Marcel Légaut gehört, von dem ich hier einen Auszug aus einem längeren Text zitiert habe, der aufgrund tiefer Naturverbundenheit enstanden ist. Marcel Légaut, ein französischer Gelehrter, Mathematiker und Philosoph, ist heute fast 90 Jahre alt. Mit 40 Jahren hatte er sein Leben vollkommen umgestellt, indem er heiratete und an der Universität von Lyon seine akademischen Titel und Ehren zurückließ. Seitdem lebt er als Landmann und Schafhirt extrem zurückgezogen auf einem hochgelegenen, einsamen Bauerngehöft in den französischen Alpen. Dort begann er zu schreiben. Worüber? ... Über Gott. Aber aus welchen Quellen, dort in dieser Abgeschiedenheit? ...

AUS DEN QUELLEN SEINER MYSTISCHEN VERSENKUNG IN DIE NATUR, in die er nunmehr eingebettet lebte und wo er zu bleiben wünschte. Heute zählt Marcel Légaut zu den großen Namen zeitgenössischer Spiritualität. Seine Bücher sind sehr reich und tief. Hören Sie ihn über sein einfaches Leben sprechen:

> Hier habe ich täglich in Symbiose gelebt,
> in Gemeinschaft mit dem, was geboren wird,
> wächst und wieder stirbt in der Stille der Natur.
> Ich bin überzeugt, daß diese Gemeinschaft etwas
> Unvergleichliches und Unersetzliches ist.
> Nichts,
> was die menschliche Gesellschaft hervorzubringen weiß,
> nichts auf dem Gebiet der höchsten Kultur
> und der edelsten Kunst, könnte mir dieses Leben
> in der Einheit mit der Natur ersetzen.

(Marcel Légaut)

Der gestreßte Großstädter unserer Zeit dagegen, der nicht von Zeit zu Zeit die Möglichkeit eines realen Kontaktes mit der Natur bekommt, dörrt innerlich aus, wird leer, das wahre Leben verläßt ihn. Ein gelegentliches Eintauchen ins ganz Naturhafte und Lebendige bedeutet ein lebensnotwendiges Auftanken für die Seele. Aus diesem Grunde baut man seit jeher Klöster an schöne Waldflecken oder Berghänge, inmitten sanfter Wiesengründe oder erquickender Wüstenoasen. Befinden sie sich aber in Städten vermauert, dann haben die Mönche oder Nonnen den Innenhof gewiß in einen lieblichen Garten verzaubert, in dem sich Geist und Seele tief erholen können. Die Natur ist fester Bestandteil des kontemplativen geistlichen Lebens, weil man dort weiß, sie ist Trägerin GÖTTLICHER BOTSCHAFTEN. Sie weist den Menschen – und hier besonders den betenden Menschen – den Weg in die heilige Dimension unseres Daseins.

Wir Alexandriner sind mit dem unermeßlichen Glück beschenkt, am Meer zu leben. Unsere Corniche, die Uferstraße, ist etwa 20 Kilometer lang, aber auch wer nicht dort wohnt, hat es nicht weit zum Strand. Den Bewohnern Alexandrias ist jederzeit dieses starke Naturerlebnis möglich, ein Rendezvous mit dem Mittelmeer in seinen ständig wechselnden Farben vom leuchtenden Kobaltblau über stechendes Türkis bis zum milchigen Rosé. Und selbst der Kontakt ist allezeit möglich, eine physische Berührung mit NATUR und GOTT durch einen Sprung in die Brandung! Welche Gnade genießen wir gegenüber den 12 Millionen Menschen im überfüllten, stickigen und staubigen Kairo! ... Und außer den endlosen, weißen Sandstränden haben wir in Alexandria erholsame Grünflächen durch Volksparks mit orientalischer Blumenkunst. Vor allem den weiten Pinienhain und die windzerzausten Seekiefern vom ausgedehnten Montazah-Gelände mit seinen idyllischen Meeresbuchten – die ehemalige Sommerresidenz König Faruks, heute allen zugänglich. Das Monstrum Kairo dagegen hat, um die Menschenmassen fassen zu können, das wenige Grün geopfert. Tausende von Häuserkasernen, Industriekomplexen und Moscheen, immer mehr von allem, und so viel Beton! Und durchdrungen sind die Wege vom Qualm der Abgase, ein höllischer Dreck überall, dauernd steigt man über Schutt und Abfälle und geht teilweise durch Kairo wie durch einen Alptraum ...

Meine lieben Freunde, die Natur hat eine humanisierende Funktion für den Menschen, und deshalb wirkt sie spiritualisierend auf ihn. Anders gesagt: Die Natur vermenschlicht, und weil sie vermenschlicht, deshalb vergeistigt sie. Jenes ZURÜCK ZUR NATUR, das sich heute fast überall regt und das sich auch zeigt an der neuen Lust am „natürlichen Urlaub" (Wandern, Klettern, Rudern, Angeln, durch die Wälder reiten, in der Wüste zelten) ist mehr als nur eine Modeerscheinung, sondern es entwächst dem tiefen Bedürfnis des heutigen Menschen nach dem ganz Ursprünglichen. In seiner technisierten, elektronisierten Lebenswelt ist er selber zum Werkzeug erstarrt und fühlt, welchen Jungbrunnen die freie Natur für ihn bedeutet. So ist es auch bewegend zu sehen, wie Städter in Hochhäusern sich aus ihrem kleinen Balkon ein liebes Gärtchen gestalteten, um diesen nötigen Kontakt mit dem Lebendigen jederzeit haben zu können.

Das Wort „Garten" ist für mich ein Zauberwort, es hat Musik für mein Ohr, denn es ruft mir Kindheitserinnerungen herbei. Ich sehe unser altes Haus in Alexandria-Ibrahemia, das wie durch ein Wunder noch immer vom Abriß verschont ist, obwohl moderne Wohnbauten das ganze Viertel völlig verändert haben. Gehe ich heute durch die Port-Said-Straße und komme dort, gleich ein paar Meter links hinter dem Rond Point an unserem ehemaligen Haus vorüber, dann bleibe ich stehen. „Unser Garten!" ... – und ich sehe mich als Junge dort bei dem allabendlichen Gaudi des Wassersprengens. Ich sehe unsere Beete wieder, die Einfassung mit den Stiefmütterchen, die hübsche pastellfarbene Wicke, die Geranien an der Treppe in ihren schweren Farben. Die zarten Stengel der hohen Papyrus-Stauden hatten den kleinen Wasserhahn, der Tag und Nacht rann, ganz verschlungen. Und mit den Obstbäumen gab es viel Spaß und Schelte für uns Kinder, weil wir in keinem Jahr die Reife abgewartet haben. Granatäpfel, Aprikosen, die beiden süßen arabischen Früchte Kichta und Guaffa, eine große starke und eine dünne Dattelpalme, und schließlich der wilde feuerlodernde Flamboyant! ... Eine solche Gartenwirklichkeit ist zugleich voller Geheimnisse – das Mysterium der Natur! Ich sehe auch das einfallende Licht und die wandernden Schatten über den Beeten, ich sehe alle vertraulichen Ecken des Gartens wieder mit ihren dicken Büschen und Sträuchern, und am Morgen die feinen Gräser über der noch atmenden Erde. Berühren wir sie, dann fällt leuchtender Tau über unsere Hand – und wir wissen, was FRIEDEN ist.

Aber auch andere Gärten kann man lieben, fremde Gärten in fremden Straßen! Jeder hat seinen Charakter, seine persönliche Note. In Europa und Amerika betreibt man in den Vororten der großen Städte oder in den Villengegenden hingebungsvolle Gartenkunst. Wohl umhegt und sauber ist es das kleine Paradies seines Besitzers, der jeden Flecken darin liebt und der sich diese Liebe manche Mühe und viel Zeit kosten läßt. Während meiner Studienjahre in diesen Ländern ist es eine meiner Freuden gewesen, durch stille Straßen mit solchen Gärten zu schlendern, deren Charme mich faszinierte und mein Herz erreichte – als ein Gleichnis ...

Und noch ein anders Naturphänomen ist für mich wichtig, und da ich auch durch dieses einst zum Gottesmysterium geführt wurde, bin ich sehr empfänglich dafür geblieben. Es ist das Erlebnis des sehr frühen Morgens. Interessanterweise hat das ein Film bei mir fertiggebracht, den ich mit 17 Jahren gesehen hatte: Der frühe Morgen war in solcher Pracht gezeigt worden, daß er für mich zur religiösen Offenbarung wurde. Seitdem ist für mich jeder Sonnenaufgang eine Epiphanie des ewigen Schöpfers, eine Erscheinung des ewig jungen Gottes.

Dieser Film zeigte eine Gruppe von Jugendlichen, die gegen fünf Uhr morgens aus ihren Häusern kamen und zusammen an einem Kanal entlang liefen, beide Ufer mit Bäumen bestanden, deren Gegenbilder wie Scherenschnitte im Licht des Wassers tanzten. Die Sonne war noch nicht zu sehen, und doch lag ihre ganze Kraft schon über der Erde. Der Horizont badete in einem so unbeschreiblichen Licht, daß ich es bis heute nicht vergessen habe. Es entwickelte sich mehr und mehr in diesem Zwischenreich – nicht mehr Nacht und noch nicht Tag – und ich fühlte mich vollkommen hineingenommen in dieses große Geheimnis des frühen Morgens. Ich verstand ihn als Weltbeginn, als leuchtende Schöpfungsstunde. Geladen voller Versprechen ist ein Morgen! Geladen von Zukunft und Hoffnung! ... Wenn ich es heute fertigbringe, um diese Uhrzeit einen Spaziergang zu machen, dann empfinde ich genau dasselbe wie damals in diesem Film vor so langer Zeit. Ich denke, wenn wir in unserem Leben etwas in seiner ganzen Tiefe erfaßt und verstanden haben, dann erkennen wir seinen geheimnistragenden Inhalt jederzeit wieder. Wir werden dieselbe Erfahrung in derselben Fülle wieder machen können – in der Ahnung der Ewigkeit ...

Ich habe, um hier nur zwei ganz persönliche Beispiele zu geben, vom GARTEN und vom FRÜHEN MORGEN gesprochen – für mich wichtige Begriffe, die zu Referenzen wurden für mein Leben, gespeist aus dem ersten starken Erlebnis. Die ganze Bibel ist eine solche Einladung zur persönlichen Gottesbegegnung anhand der Weltrealität mit allen Kreaturen, von denen jede eine lebendige Hymne zur Verherrlichung des Schöpfers darstellt. „Die Himmel rühmen Gottes Ehre, das Sternengewölbe kündet seiner Hände Werk ...", singt der Psalmist.

Lobpreist den Herrn, du Sonne und du Mond!
Lobpreist Ihn all ihr hellen Sterne! ...
Lobpreist den Herrn, die ihr auf Erden weilet,
ihr Meerestiere all, ihr Meeresfluten ...

Ihr Bergeshöhen all, ihr Hügel!
Du Wild und all ihr zahmen Tiere!
Gewürm und ihr beschwingten Vögel!
Ihr Erdenkönige, ihr Völker all!
Ihr Fürsten alle und ihr Erdenrichter!
Ihr Greise und ihr Jungen,
Lobpreisen sollen sie des Herren Namen!

(Psalm 148)

Wer diese Sprache des Universums zu lesen versteht, dem ist die Natur eine unversiegelte Schrift, ein offenes und einladendes Buch, das ihm zur „Heiligen Schrift" werden kann, zur Bibel vor der Bibel, die großartig und unerschöpflich von Gottes Schöpfungstun berichtet. So schrieb auch Paulus an die Römer:

Denn was an Gott erkennbar ist, ist ihnen wohlbekannt. Gott selber hat es ihnen ja geoffenbart. Was an ihm unsichtbar ist, wird in den Geschöpfen durch Nachdenken seit Erschaffung der Welt bekannt: Seine ewige Allmacht und Göttlichkeit. Darum sind sie unentschuldbar, denn sie erkannten zwar Gott, verherrlichten ihn aber nicht als Gott und dankten ihm nicht. Vielmehr gerieten sie mit ihrem Denken auf Torheiten, und ihr unverständiges Herz ward verfinstert. Sie gaben sich als Weise aus und waren doch Toren geworden.

(Römer 1, 19-22)

Der Weise hört jede einzelne Gottesschöpfung als Zeile einer Hymne, als eine Melodie der großen Weltsymphonie: Eine stille Musik ist es, eine wortlose Sprache; die Natur spricht lautlos zu uns, doch „vernehmlich" ...

Nicht Reden sind's, nicht Worte, die nicht vernehmlich klängen, ihr Schall durchtönt die ganze Erde, und ihre Laute dringen bis zum Rand der Welt.

(Psalm 19)

In den großen Psalmengesängen ist es bald das ganze Himmelszelt, das anstimmt zum „wunderbaren Lobgesang", bald sind es Meer, Wind und Wolken mit ihren Regengüssen für die Erde, Berge und Täler, die Wälder mit ihren Vögeln, die Flüsse mit allem Getier, kurz: Es sind JUBELGESÄNGE der gesamten Schöpfung, die sich im einzelnen ihres Ursprungs wohl bewußt ist.

Dem Herrn sagt Dank! Verherrlicht Seinen Namen!
Kund machet Seine Taten den Nationen!
Lobsingt von Ihm! Lobt Ihn!
Erzählt von Seinen Wundern all!

(Psalm 105)

Zu den Psalmenmelodien gehört auch ein großes Preislied, das im Prophetenbuch Daniel zwei Seiten einnimmt. Es ist der dreistimmige Lobgesang von drei Verurteilten des Königs Nebukadnezar, gesungen aus der Glut eines flammentobenden Feuerofens, „angeschürt mit Naphta, Reisig und Pech, sodaß die Flammen 49 Ellen über den Ofen in die Höhe schlugen". Sie aber besangen darin Gottes Weisheit, Gerechtigkeit, Heiligkeit und Herrlichkeit, und das Feuer konnte die gottesfürchtigen Männer nicht erreichen. Die ganze Schöpfung der Natur gehen sie im einzelnen durch und fordern alles, auch das Kleinste, zum Lobpreis Gottes auf.

Denken wir ferner an das alttestamentarische Lehrbuch JOB, und lesen wir am Ende den großen Monolog Gottes gegenüber dem verzweifelt fragenden Job. Um ihm endlich seine Güte, Allmacht und unendliche Weisheit begreiflich zu machen, offenbart Gott sich ihm als Schöpfungsprinzip. Er entfaltet dem Menschen das grandiose Fresko seiner Schöpfung. Der Autor dieses Textes verwendet einen so unübertroffenen Stil, daß dieses biblische Buch zu den Meisterwerken der Weltliteratur gerechnet wird. Man lese besonders seine letzten Kapitel 38-41. Gott geht hier bis ins Detail in seiner Weltbeschreibung, er erwähnt selbst die kleinen Eiskristalle und den Tau und spricht von „der Wolken Weisheit". Und er stellt dem Job fortwährend Fragen wie diese:

Wer gibt dem Raben seine Atzung,
wenn seine Jungen schrein zu Mir
und ohne Nahrung flattern?

Das Nilpferd sieh dir an, das Ich erschaffen
im Vergleich zu dir! ...
Betrachte doch die Kraft in seinen Lenden,

seine Beine sind wie Eisenstäbe
und Lotosbüschel überdachen es als Schattenspender,
des Baches Weiden halten es umfangen.
Wenn sich ein Strom ergießt, wird ihm nicht bange,
es bleibt getrost, ergösse sich ein Jordan ihm ins Maul.

Verleihest du dem Rosse Heldenkraft,
bekleidest seinen Hals mit einer Mähne,
bewirkest, daß es wie ein Rauchfang dampfe?
Erschreckend ist sein mächtig Wiehern,
voll Freude springt es in das Tal,
voll Kraft stürzt es den Harnischen entgegen,
von Ferne wittert es den Streit.

(Job 38, 39, 40)

Jede Kreatur kündet auf ihre besondere Weise von der Größe Gottes, und es genügt schon, sich in einen kleinen Teilaspekt der Natur zu versenken, um zu fühlen, wie sich das eigene Herz zu Gott erhebt. In dieser „Herzerhebung" sind die Psalmenlieder geschaffen worden. Auch der Koran ist sehr reich durchzogen von großartigen Texten dieser Art zum Preise Allahs, des Weltenschöpfers. Und welchen weisen Rat gibt uns die Gestalt eines alten Eremiten aus der russischen Literatur?

> Liebt die ganze Schöpfung Gottes, liebt alles bis zum letzten Staubkorn! Wenn Ihr alles liebt, dann werdet Ihr das Gottesmysterium in allem erkennen.

(Dostojevski)

Darin liegt der ganze Unterschied zwischen wissenschaftlicher Forschungsarbeit und mystischer Betrachtung. Der Wissenschaftler konstatiert die sichtbaren Welterscheinungen und analysiert sie gründlich, er legt sie auseinander und dann wieder zusammen. Dann beschreibt er präzise den Vorgang und stellt heraus, was seine Augen beobachtet haben. Dieser Blick ist durchdringend, suchend und pragmatisch. Der Mystiker hat andere Ziele und andere Methoden. Er geht vor allem mit einer stark liebenden Seele auf seine Suche, ja in verliebter Haltung! Sein Blick beschränkt sich niemals auf äußerlich sichtbare Zusammenhänge, sondern er will mehr, er dringt tiefer ein, und er tastet sich bis ins Innerste vor. Er sucht das

Wesen der Dinge zu ergründen. Weil er sie von Herzen liebt, deshalb sucht er ihr Herz! Was Dostojevski „das Gottesgeheimnis in allem" nennt, das findet auch der Mystiker in seiner Tiefenschau und Liebesschau. Sein Blick erfährt das innere Sichtbarwerden des Wesentlichen, das dem gewöhnlichen Blick im allgemeinen verhüllt bleibt, denn

> man sieht nur mit dem Herzen gut,
> das Wesentliche ist für die Augen unsichtbar.
>
> (Saint-Exupéry)

Ein russischer und ein französischer Dichter! Beide formulierten in treffender Weise diese Wahrheit, jeder auf seine Art. Dazu empfehle ich Ihnen noch etwas aus meiner persönlichen Erfahrung und Praxis: Gehen Sie durch die Welt wie durch einen Garten, der Ihnen gehört! Sagen Sie sich: „Die Welt ist Gottes Welt, und deshalb ist es auch die meine. Gott hat mich als sein Kind gewollt und als seinen Erben eingesetzt." Deshalb verwendete Jesus in seinem Gleichnis vom Verlorenen Sohn die Vaterworte:

> *Mein Sohn, du bist allezeit bei mir,*
> *und all das Meinige ist dein.*
>
> (Lukas 15, 31)

Dasselbe lesen wir in zwei Paulusbriefen:

> *So seid ihr denn nicht mehr Fremde und Beisassen,*
> *sondern Mitbürger der Heiligen und Hausgenossen*
> *Gottes.*
>
> (Epheser 1, 19)

> *Weil ihr nun Söhne seid, so sandte Gott in unsere*
> *Herzen den Geist seines Sohnes, und dieser ruft:*
> *„Abba! Lieber Vater!" So bist du also nicht mehr Knecht,*
> *sondern Sohn, wenn aber Sohn, dann Erbe durch Gott.*
>
> (Galater 4, 6-7)

Aufgrund meiner GOTTESKINDSCHAFT erbe ich die ganze Welt, als KIND GOTTES besitze ich die ganze Erde! Alles gehört mir, der helle Frühlingswald, das weite Meer und das auf ganz wunderbare Weise geordnete Universum – alles gehört mir!

Die Mystiker, die sich in vollkommener Entäußerung willentlich verarmt hatten, schwelgten letztlich in der Fülle des Gefühls, daß ihnen alles gehöre. Alles! Sie besaßen nichts und doch alles, sie hatten alles verlieren wollen und dabei alles gewonnen. Wieder erinnere ich an Franz von Assisi und Johannes vom Kreuz: Ihre hymnischen Gebete künden davon, daß sie im höchsten Maß ihr Herz von allem befreit hatten, um eines Tages sagen zu können: „Himmel und Erde sind mein, Sonne, Mond und Sterne sind mein, die ganze Welt ist mein."

Wer von Ihnen keinen Garten besitzt, der möge die Natur als sein Eigentum betrachten. Wer kein eigenes Haus bewohnt, der nehme die ganze Welt dafür. Und wer keine Familie sein eigen nennen kann, dem werde die ganze Menschheit zur Familie. In den Seligpreisungen der Bergpredigt hat Christus die Armen angesprochen und sie reich gemacht:

Selig, ihr Armen, denn euer ist das Reich Gottes.

(Lukas 6, 20)

Es liegt eine seltsame Wahrheit um die Armut. Innere Armut führt uns gerade zu den außerordentlichsten und undenkbarsten Reichtümern und zum ganzen Weltbesitz, „ ... dann werden wir fähig sein, das Universum keusch zu umarmen" – die Sprache Teilhard de Chardins! Für den Mystiker bildet der Himmel und die Erde ein geschlossenes Ganzes, es ist ein Reich, das EINE!

Die jenseitige Welt ist nichts anderes
als die Tiefe dieser Welt.

(Dostojevski)

Nein, die andere Welt ist nicht woanders, sondern hier bei uns – in uns. Sie ist die Tiefendimension unserer Welt. Hier wird unser Blick auf das Tabor-Ereignis gelenkt, man nennt es „Christi Verklärung", und in diesem Tabor-Licht verstehen wir das bisher Gesagte besser:

Christus nahm sich drei Jünger seiner Wahl mit auf einen hohen, abseits gelegenen Berg namens Tabor, um zu beten. Dort offenbarte er ihnen sein inneres Wesen, doch nicht in Worten, sondern in einer geistigen Schau, und *„sie sahen Seine Herrlichkeit"* (Lukas 9). Dieser verklärte Leib Christi, den sie plötzlich wahrnehmen durften, war derselbe Leib, der mit ihnen täglich über die Straßen Palästinas wanderte, der Nahrung und Wasser aufnahm wie sie, die Jünger. Hier aber erschien ihnen plötzlich ein ganz anderer Leib ihres Meisters. Was war geschehen? Eine Erscheinung hatte stattgefunden, eine neue, andere Erscheinung, aber desselben Christus, den sie alle Tage sahen und erlebten, der sich von ihm in keiner Weise wesensmäßig unterschied! Jetzt hatte er die Jünger von einem Moment zum andern seine bisher verhüllte Transzendenz schauen lassen und ihnen sein Mysterium offenbart.

> *Und er ward verwandelt vor ihnen ... Seine Kleider wurden schimmernd weiß, wie sie kein Walker auf der Erde bleichen kann ... Sie waren vor Schrecken außer sich.*
>
> (aus Markus 9)

> *Sein Antlitz glänzte wie die Sonne, und seine Kleider wurden leuchtend wie das Licht.*
>
> (Matthäus 17, 2)

Augenblicke der Gnade! ... Vorübergehend, für eine gnadenvolle Zeit, durften sie diese Einsicht in ihn gewinnen. Christus hatte den äußeren Schleier der Materie von sich weggezogen und seine innere Wirklichkeit erkennen lassen, die ihnen bisher verborgen geblieben war. Sein Wesen, sein Lichtwesen, strahlte so hell, daß sie „vor Schrecken außer sich waren".

Solche Tabor-Erfahrungen können auch wir haben. Es geschieht immer dann, wenn wir die Herrlichkeit Gottes im gewöhnlichen Alltag sicher erkennen, wenn dieses Wissen durchbricht wie ein Lichtstrahl und alles Leben für einen Augenblick anhält und verklärt. So wie ein schattendunkles Kirchenfenster, das, plötzlich vom starken Sonnenstrahl getroffen, sich wandelt in ein farbsprühendes Feuerwerk ...

Nachdem das WORT Fleisch geworden ist, hat es nicht mehr aufgehört, diese Welt zu bewohnen und alle Dinge und Wesen, die sie enthält, drücken dieses Mysterium aus. Deshalb müssen wir im Gebet auf die heimliche Stimme der Dinge achten, um ihre Existenz auf das WORT zurückzuführen, ihren Ursprung, ihr Leben.

Die Dinge sprechen nicht, sie sind ganz zufrieden damit, nur zu sein. Aber ihr Sein ist schon ein Wort, das sich in der Stille an uns richtet. Derjenige, der es versteht, der Welt in der rechten Haltung zu begegnen, wird eine Offenbarung des göttlichen Wortes erleben können. Es zeigt sich uns in der Ruhe und im Geheimen, in der Bescheidenheit eines grünen Blattes mit dem winzigen Insekt darauf; sie beide besingen durch ihr Da-Sein, durch ihre Existenz den Schöpfer. Beide sind Abbilder des Gottesmysteriums.

Man findet Gott in der Natur, man findet ihn im Wahren und Schönen. Im SCHÖNEN wahrscheinlich noch tiefer und existenzieller. Leider haben wir uns von einem massiven Intellektualismus stark verbilden lassen. Wir wollen Ideen, immer mehr Ideen, und wir produzieren Wörter, immer mehr Wörter, wo doch das Gebet gerade das Gegenteil ist! Je mehr Ideen sich sammeln und Worte sich finden, umso weniger betet die Seele. BETEN heißt, aus seinem Wesen wieder eine Einheit schaffen. Die Idee vereint nicht unser Wesen, denn sie steht uns gegenüber und argumentiert, sie lebt getrennt von uns. Wir glauben zu sehr, Gott in einem Ideennetz einfangen zu können und ihn durch logisches Diskutieren zu bestimmen und festzulegen. Aber welch tiefer Abstand besteht zwischen der höchsten Theologie und der einfachen Mystik! Hier haben wir zwei verschiedene Ordnungen, deren Wege teilweise sogar auseinanderlaufen. Gott bleibt immer jenseits unserer spitzfindigsten Gedanken und geschliffenen Wortmanifestationen. Gerade das, was man bei solchen Gelegenheiten durch Worte zusammendrängt, ist noch längst nicht Gott, sondern etwas ganz anderes.

Der hl. Ignatius von Loyola hatte bald nach seiner Bekehrung ein Jahr in einer Höhle bei Manresa verbracht und in der Stille dieser grandiosen Natur sein Leben umgestellt. Dort, oberhalb des Cardoner-Flusses, wurde ihm sein großes Erleuchtungserlebnis zuteil. Er machte tiefe Erfahrungen über die Geheimnisse der Schöpfung und der Dreifaltigkeit, gewann Erkenntnis über die Glaubenszusammenhänge und das geistliche Leben in allen Einzelheiten. Und wieviel mag er uns in seinen persönlichen Aufzeichnungen über diese entscheidende Stunde seines Lebens hinterlassen haben? Nur ein paar magere Zeilen, eigentlich kaum etwas! Das könnte man sonderbar finden, ganz unerklärlich sogar, gar nicht im Verhältnis stehend zur Bedeutung, die es für sein späteres Leben hatte. Lesen wir, was der Heilige als Substanz notiert hat:

> Innerhalb weniger Augenblicke wurde mir die Offenbarung des trinitarischen Geheimnisses zuteil und zwar in einer solchen Klarheit und Tiefe, daß alles, was ich bis zu diesem Tag darüber gehört und gelesen hatte, worüber ich meditiert hatte, womit ich meine Theologie und Spiritualität gespeist hatte, und all das, was noch auf mich zukam an neuer Erkenntnislehre über Gott und die Dreifaltigkeit, sich zu einem Nichts zusammenzieht, wenn ich es in Beziehung setze zur Erkenntnis dieses einen Tages.
>
> (Ignatius von Loyola)

Das Erlebte war unsagbar. Er hatte es nicht in Worte kleiden können, nicht einmal für sich persönlich, weil es keine Worte dafür gab. Das Gottesmysterium, wie das Mysterium des Seins, ist unsagbar – aber es ist erfühlbar, erschaubar, klar erlebbar. Hier hat zweifellos die Schönheit ihren Anteil, ihre Rolle als Botschaftsträger. In seinem Fall vielleicht die Schönheit jener Flußlandschaft bei Manresa ...

Die Knechtschaft unserer abstrakten Gedanken- und Ideenwelt müssen wir unbedingt verlassen, in die unsere Epoche bestrebt ist, uns einzuschließen. Was man in einer bestimmten Tiefenzone seines Wesens erlebt, wird einem immer unsagbar bleiben. Man lebt es, und das ist genug. Man wird erfüllt davon, und das genügt! Es ist, als ob das Unendliche als Lichtflut in uns einfiele, die uns von innen ganz erhellt. Das mag das Schöne bewirken! Ein Einsinken ins Mysterium des Seins, das ganz aus Licht besteht. Erlebbar, doch ganz unsagbar.

Das wirklich Schöne gibt ja doch das Wahre frei, da es einen Durchbruch durch die Hülle der Dinge bedeutet. Betrachten Sie eine Blume – sie IST. Sie spricht nicht zu Ihnen, doch ihre Gegenwart ist eine Sprache. Wenn ich bei ihr verweile und ihr meine ganze Aufmerksamkeit schenke, dann wird diese Blumenexistenz zur Sprache werden, die sich an mich wendet. Kontemplieren bedeutet, sich in das Wesen der Dinge versenken, um ihr Geheimnis zu erfahren, das sie uns mitteilen möchten.

Jede Wirklichkeit gibt einerseits ihr Geheimnis preis und andererseits verbirgt sie es vor uns ... Sie öffnet sich, doch nicht in der Art einer vollen Entblößung, denn indem sie sich hingibt, behält sie doch ihr Geheimstes ein ... Daher geschieht es, daß man bei der Entdeckung der Wesen zwar weit, sehr weit gehen kann, ohne je eine Grenze zu berühren und mit ihnen an ein Ende zu kommen. Deshalb sprechen wir ja vom GEHEIMNIS der Wesen, von ihrem Mysterium, weil es eben unerschöpflich für uns bleibt, denn es gibt sich und bleibt doch letztlich unerreichbar.

Das Geheimnis des wirklich Schönen liegt gerade in seiner Unerschöpflichkeit, es ist unerschöpflich reich wie eine Quelle. Eine Schönheit, von der man sagen kann, man habe sie „ausgekostet", war keine wahre Schönheit, sondern nur ein Abglanz, eine Ahnung. Ausschöpfen und auskosten kann man nur flüchtige Schönheiten. Nehmen Sie dagegen am Beispiel des Menschen das Gesicht der Maria des Fra Angelico, und betrachten Sie es gut. Sie werden sich für Stunden in dieses Gemälde einleben können, denn das Mariengesicht bleibt unerschöpflich! Hier erfahren Sie eine wahre Schönheit, die sich freizügig hingibt und doch zugleich einbehält.

Hierzu ein großer Grieche des 4. Jahrhunderts:

> Steht einer an einer Quelle und staunt über das
> entspringende Wasser, wird er sagen, er habe all
> ihr Wasser gesehen? Auch wenn er lange am Ent-
> springen verweilt, so bleibt er doch immer am
> Anfang seines Schauens. Immer ist die Quelle im
> Ursprung. So ergeht es auch dem, der auf die
> göttliche, grenzenlose Schönheit blickt.
> Niemals hört die Sehnsucht nach dem Schauen auf,
> denn das über dem Gefundenen Erahnte
> ist immer noch größer und göttlicher
> als alles Erschaute.

(Gregor von Nyssia)

Auch die Natur zeigt und verbirgt uns ihr Wesen. Deshalb sprechen wir ja vom GEHEIMNIS DER NATUR. Durch sie geht ein Zug von Schüchternheit oder Schamhaftigkeit, weil sie beides will, sie will sich uns zeigen und verschwinden zugleich. Das ist ihr Mysterium ...

Die Tiefe der wahren Naturschönheit ist im Einfachsten und Gewöhnlichsten unserer Umgebung zu finden. Manche unter uns müssen allerdings erst am Ufer des Comer Sees stehen oder ein teures

Hotelfenster öffnen mit Blick auf das Montblanc-Massiv, um das Schöne begeistert zu preisen. Sie müssen lange Flugstrecken zurücklegen mit Kurs auf die Touristenzentren der Superlative, um dort, und nur dort, das Schöne zu finden. Bedauernswerte Leute! ... Wem es aber gelingt, einem kleinen Pflänzchen längere Zeit zuzuschauen, wie es sich im Morgenwinde wiegt, dem genügt dieses Erleben des Schönen. Auch ein Vöglein genügt, das von Ihrem Fenstersims pickt, denn das Schöne summiert sich alle Tage um uns her! Haben wir die Augen dafür? Warum überlassen wir den „gewissen Blick" denn nur den Künstlern? Er sieht gut! Das Alltägliche ist für ihn schon eine Öffnung zum Unendlichen hin, deshalb ist er fähig, aus einer Steingruppierung um eine Wasserpfütze ein Meisterwerk zu machen.

Überall und allezeit umgibt uns die Schönheit. Wenn wir uns den Blick für sie erwerben, dann hören wir auch endlich auf, die Erde als „unmenschlich" und „gottverlassen" zu verkünden. Plötzlich rücken uns die Dinge und Wesen sehr vertraulich nahe, ans Herz rücken sie uns, und wir gehen gern und liebevoll mit ihnen um. Ein lebendiger Austausch beginnt, jetzt besteht GEMEINSCHAFT. Die Natur wird mir dann zur Freundin, zur intimen Vetrauten, mit der ich mich im innigen Dialog befinde in Liebe vereint.

Die Welt wirbt um diesen Austausch mit dem Menschen. Sie strebt danach und bittet darum, sich ihm hinzugeben, wie ein junges Mädchen danach strebt, sich dem Geliebten hinzugeben. Die Welt strebt zu dieser Gemeinschaft, die sie mit dem Menschen feiern will, sie will sich mit ihm vereinen wie in einer hochzeitlichen Bindung, denn sie sucht die wahre Liebesbeziehung. Sie sucht sie mit Ihnen, und sie sucht sie mit mir. Sprechen Sie daher die leisen Worte: „An mir liegt es. Es bleibt mir nur, die Arme zu öffnen und mein Herz bereit zu machen, um die Welt in mich einzulassen. Wenn ich mit der Fülle der Welt kommuniziere, dann kommuniziere ich mit der Fülle des Gottesmysteriums."

Ich schließe mit einigen Zeilen aus meinen persönlichen Aufzeichnungen aus der Zeit meiner Studienjahre zum Themenkreis „Gebet und Kontemplation":

> Das konkrete, reale, existenzielle Gebet
> führt von den sichtbaren Dingen zu den unsichtbaren;
> vom materiellen Sein zum immateriellen Sein,

welches im Höchstmaß real ist.
Es führt vom Wesen des Wahrnehmbaren
zur höchsten Wesenheit.

Die Worte des Universums hören lernen!
Das Geheimnis der Welt schauen lernen!
Die Harmonie der Dinge und Wesen erkennen!

Diese herrliche Symphonie im Geheimnis
ihrer Einfachheit und Alltäglichkeit
verstehen und genießen lernen!

Herr, lehre mich die Sprache der Welt verstehen.
Schenke mir den Schlüssel,
der mir zum Allerheiligsten Eintritt gewährt.
Dort, im Innersten des Seins,
werde ich Erfahrungen machen,
die keine Zunge sprechen kann,
da keine Sprache sie kennt.
Es wird noch mehr für mich sein als eine Schau:
Es wird ein Mahl werden!
Noch mehr: Eine Umarmung!
Noch mehr: Eine Hochzeit! ...
Einswerdung mit dem Mysterium der Wesen.

Original:
Le Mystère de la Nature. Pour une mystique d' incarnation
(Kairo/Ägypten 1986)

Haben die Dinge einen Sinn?

Jedes leibliche, materielle Sein drückt in seiner Stofflichkeit das aus, was es im Innersten und im Wesentlichen ist. Alle Materie verbirgt während der Zeit, in der sie sich manifestiert, einen Sinn. Jeder Leib verbirgt während der Zeit seiner Existenz eine Seele.

Die Materie ist eine Idee, die einen Leib annimmt. Durch diesen Akt wird sie zum Zeichen und zur Offenbarung dieser Idee, die ihr Zentrum bildet. Jedes materielle Sein ist Ausdruck eines Sinnes, seine Bedeutung wird sichtbar. Es ist das Äußere eines Inneren, oder, wie man sagt, das Phänomen eines Noumenon, das heißt des im Innern verborgenen Wesentlichen.

Aber Leib und Materie sind nicht nur die Erscheinungen der Dinge im Raum, sie existieren noch in einer anderen Dimension: in der Zeit. Die Manifestation der Dinge in der Zeit betrifft ihre Wirksamkeit und damit ihre Geschichte. Man kann ein materielles Sein nur in seiner Dauer verstehen, denn im gegebenen Augenblick bleibt es ein Rätsel für uns. Wirklich manifestiert es sich nur in seiner Bewegungstendenz, seinem Wirken, seiner Geschichte.

Demnach ist die Geschichte nicht nur Vergangenheit, sondern auch Zukunft. Und diese Zukunft ist gerade das wesentliche Element, denn nur in der Zielsetzung versteht man alle Bewegung. War die Vergangenheit denn nicht der Beginn einer Bewegung, die an ihr zukünftiges Ziel gekommen ist?

Um ein Ding ganz zu erfassen, muß man gut verstehen, wohin es strebt und was es werden soll. Was ist seine Berufung und damit seine tiefe Endgültigkeit? Dieses Letzte heißt es zu ergründen, die eigentliche Bedeutung des materiellen Seins. Freilich ist uns jene Zukunft unbekannt, wäre es aber nicht doch möglich, sie aus der Vergangenheit herzuleiten? Würde ein ernstes und genaues Studium nicht sinnbringend sein, uns diese Richtung wenigstens anzuzeigen, in die alles zielt, und aus der wir das Kommende abzulesen vermögen?

Fragen wir doch die Vergangenheit, was sie uns lehrt! Sie sagt, daß die Dinge zurückgelassene Teile während des Aufstiegs zum Menschen sind (vgl. Teilhard de Chardin). Sie sagt, daß der Sinn der Dinge darin besteht, daß diese Gesamtbewegung nur in einen einzigen Punkt von Raum und Zeit einmünden kann – in den Menschen! Nach dem Menschen also, ihrem letzten Sinn und Ziel, streben die Dinge und sehnen sich nach dieser Vereinigung, doch sind sie nicht fähig, dieses Ziel auf der reinen Linie ihrer natürlichen Entwicklung zu erreichen. Dieses Schöpfungswunder hat in der Entwicklungsgeschichte nur ein einziges Mal stattgefunden, und es wird sich wohl kaum wiederholen.

Es ist also der Mensch, der die Dinge zu ihrer Bestimmung führt, indem er sie assimiliert. Der Mensch trägt die Dinge ihrem wahren Ziel entgegen, indem er sie zu seinem Besten nutzt, indem er sie sich unterwirft – *„Macht euch die Erde untertan! Herrschet!"* (Genesis 1) – und ihnen damit ihren Existenzsinn verleiht. Somit verwirklicht er ihre Berufung.

Es geht also nicht darum, den Sinn der Dinge theoretisch zu erforschen, sondern ihnen einen Sinn zu geben, und dieser besteht darin, den inneren Menschen heranzubilden. Menschliche Arbeit und die Veränderung der Welt ist also nicht die Vergewaltigung und Ausbeutung der Dinge, sondern im Gegenteil, es bedeutet für sie Förderung und Aufstieg in eine höhere Ordnung als die ihre. Nach diesem höheren Standort sehnen sich die Dinge, können diesen Entwicklungsschritt aus sich heraus aber nicht vollziehen.

Was wir über die menschliche Arbeit sagen, kann ebenso von zwei anderen Daseinsbereichen gesagt werden, über das niedere und über das höhere Niveau menschlichen Lebens:

Auf dem niederen Niveau haben wir die Ernährung. Durch sie nimmt der Mensch das Mineral, die Pflanze und das Tier in einer höheren Synthese in sich auf, und das Leben transzendiert in den Bereich des menschlichen Denkens und Empfindens, des Geistes und des Gefühls. Die Dinge „fühlen" diese Aufstiegsmöglichkeit und befinden sich deshalb in einem ständigen Spannungszustand auf den Menschen hin, er ist ihre innere Richtung und ihr Ziel. Sie haben daher nur den einen Wunsch, von ihm aufgenommen und assimiliert zu werden, um damit zu ihrer wahren Bestimmung aufzusteigen, zu ihrer Verwirklichung.

Auf dem höheren Niveau haben wir die geistige Erkenntnis, die Kunst und die Kontemplation. Durch diese spirituellen Tätigkeiten wird die Welt in eine wirklich menschliche Sphäre versetzt und erreicht eine neue, eine höhere Dimension – die des Geistes.

Durch das Aufnehmen der Dinge durch den Menschen sind die Dinge jetzt humanisiert worden und finden einen Sinn – ihren Sinn. Könnten wir hier nicht hinzusetzen, daß alles menschliche Streben, das über sich hinauszielt, alle Askese und alle anderen Formen des Sich-Besiegens und des Herr-Werdens über unsere Triebwelt schließlich die entscheidensten Etappen in der Humanisierung unserer Welt bedeuten? Denn erst über Arbeit, Kunst und Erkenntnis hinaus findet in unserem Innern die endgültige Partie statt: Die Vermenschlichung unserer „Natur", d. h. die Vergeistigung des inneren Tieres. Das Werk der Vergeistigung und der Heiligwerdung ist demnach die vollkommenste und entscheidenste Form menschlicher Arbeit; hier geschieht das Wesentliche und Letztgültige, und aller Rest ist von sekundärer Bedeutung. Gewiß gilt sein Wert der notwendigen Suche, doch das innere Werden betreffend bleibt es unzureichend.

Diese Selbstüberwindung, die dem Menschen in seinem Herzen gelingt, indem er vom Fleisch-Menschen zum Geist-Menschen aufsteigt, ist nichts anderes als seine letzte Etappe: die Christwerdung. Hier erhalten Dinge und Mensch gemeinsam ihren wahren und endgültigen Sinn. Hier liegt das Ziel aller Bewegung, die Rückkehr der Schöpfung an ihren Ausgangspunkt.

Der Sinn der Dinge liegt also in ihrer Selbstüberwindung zum Menschen hin. Und der Sinn des Menschen liegt in seiner Selbstüberwindung zu Christus hin ...

Der letzte Sinn liegt für beide, für die Dinge wie für den Menschen, im Heraustreten aus sich selbst, um damit ein Höheres und Größeres zu erreichen, als sie selber sind. All das zeigt, daß der Sinn allen Seins nicht zu suchen ist, sondern er muß eigens vollbracht werden.

Original:
Les choses, ont-elles un sens?
(Alexandria/Ägypten 1978)

Christlicher Humanismus

Der Mensch ist Geist, das heißt, er verspürt Verlangen nach dem Unendlichen und besitzt auch die Fähigkeit, es zu erreichen und in ihm aufzugehen. Nichts anderes bestimmt unser Leben als diese lange Suche, dieses tiefe Fragen und Forschen nach dem Unendlichen, das uns ganz erfüllen soll.

Ganz erfüllen? ... Vollkommen erreichen wir dieses Ziel erst, nachdem wir einer radikalen Wesensverwandlung unterzogen wurden. Diese Umwandlung erfahren wir im Augenblick unseres Todes, sie bringt uns in den Besitz dieses höchsten Gutes. Doch in Erwartung dieses letzten Augenblicks müssen wir uns gut auf diese Begegnung vorbereiten, denn sie ist nun einmal das Endziel des geistigen Menschenwesens, das Ziel seiner Lebensstrecke. Diese Begegnung dürfen wir herzlich herbeiwünschen und sollen uns ihrer würdig erweisen, wenn es soweit ist.

Die große Versuchung für den Menschen besteht jedoch darin, daß er sein Leben lang den Durst nach dem Unendlichen anderweitig und vor der Zeit zu stillen bestrebt ist. In der fortwährenden Illusion befangen, sucht er sein höheres Verlangen nach dem Unendlichen mit Endlichem zu befriedigen. Aber, ob er es immer weiß oder nicht, es ist der Hunger nach Gott, der seine Seele so bewegt und ihn nach allen Richtungen und auf alle Weisen nach ihm suchen läßt. Irrtümlich will sich der Mensch am Geschaffenen und Endlichen sättigen, er will aufgehen im Hier und im Jetzt.

Deshalb sagt die Kirche, der Mensch „sündige", wenn er diesem Fehler unterliege: „Sündigend verletzt er Gott damit und vergeht sich zugleich gegen sich selbst. Er verletzt Gott, weil er etwas Geschaffenem den Stellenwert gibt, der nur dem Schöpfer des Geschaffenen zukommt, und er vergeht sich gegen sich selbst, weil er sich damit in einen Zustand inneren Widerspruchs gebracht hat, der jetzt störend oder zerstörend an ihm nagt."

Denn in Wahrheit versucht der Mensch das ganz Unmögliche, wenn er seine Sehnsucht nach dem Unendlichen auf etwas Endliches reduziert. Es gelingt ihm nicht, und er wird daran leiden, daß es ihm nicht gelingt. Seine Wunschverfehlung muß ihm in der Folge viel innere Spannung einbringen und manches Leiden schaffen, das wiederum viele Arten anderer Störungen nach sich zieht – Kettenreaktion! ... Andererseits, sobald sich der wohl erkennende, geistige Mensch begreift und sich nun dem Lichte Gottes zuwendet, wird ihn die Harmonie aufs neue erfüllen, und alles fügt sich in die ursprüngliche Ordnung.

Deshalb sprechen wir von der Sünde des Götzendienstes, weil hier anstelle wahrer Gotteshingabe ein Kult geübt wird. Weltliche Genüsse und anhaltende Vergnügungen, welcher Form auch immer, das Streben nach Geld, Besitz, Macht oder Ansehen sind letztlich Götzendienste. Auch die sexuelle Liebe kann als Kult geübt werden, sodaß Gott darüber vergessen wird. Das Ungute daran ist jedoch nicht unsere Liebe zur Kreatur, denn die Kreatur – im allgemeinen oder im besonderen – ist liebenswert und verdient unsere Zuneigung, aber das „Sündige" ist der Absolutheitswert, den wir dieser Neigung geben. Anders gesagt: Wir lieben etwas Endliches mit jener unendlichen und alles andere ausschließenden Seelenkraft, die nur Gott allein zukommen soll.

Doch trägt jedes Geschöpf, und besonders das menschliche, gewisse Züge seines Schöpfers, es reflektiert dieses Unendliche. Und gerade das ist es ja, das es so anziehend und liebenswert macht! Im Handumdrehen mag man fasziniert und gefesselt sein, denn das Unendliche all seiner Sehnsucht projiziert man jetzt in diese eine Person oder in diese eine Sache und glaubt mit Sicherheit, sich jetzt darin zu verwirklichen. Die Seele ergießt sich jetzt in dieses Objekt der vermeintlichen Erfüllung, und sie will ganz darin aufgehen. Das aber wird nicht möglich sein. So ist es nur eine Frage der Zeit, wann sich Bitternis und Traurigkeit im Herzen melden, wann Zweifel sich mehren und Reue aufsteigt, und wann schließlich die Erkenntnis durchschlägt, erneut am Ausgangspunkt zu stehen – vor der Leere der eigenen Seele.

Dieser „Fall des Menschen aus dem Paradies" mag jedoch eine positive Konsequenz haben, nämlich diese Erkenntnis. Jetzt versucht der Mensch einen neuen Weg, bewußt will er seine Lebensauffassung und Lebensart ändern. Er bemüht sich darum, aber vielleicht schlägt nun alles ins Gegenteil? ...

Nachdem der Mensch nach einer solchen mehr oder weniger schmerzlichen Erfahrung allem Geschöpflichen den Rücken wendet, um sich allein Gott hinzugeben, erfüllt ihn neue Hoffnung. Doch löst er damit nicht sein Problem. Die Geschöpfe werden ihn auch fernerhin verführen und seinen Geist besetzen, und sie werden sich einschleichen in seinen Leib! Es ist leider Illusion zu glauben, daß ein Willensakt genüge, um den schönen Dingen und lebendigen Wesen dieser Welt ihre Faszination nehmen zu können, denn sobald man sich von der materiellen Täuschung befreit hat, unterliegt man der geistigen.

> Der Mensch ist weder Engel noch Tier;
> das Unglück will es aber,
> daß derjenige, der sich zum Engel machen will,
> zum Tier wird.
>
> (Pascal)

Die Wahrheit liegt wie oft in der „goldenen Mitte". Sie liegt in einer bestimmten Ordnung, die eine Rangordnung ist und innere Harmonie bedeutet. Gott schließt ja doch die Geschöpfe nicht aus und die Geschöpfe nicht Gott, sondern dort in dieser Ordnung findet alles in enger Verflechtung seinen wahren Platz. Dieses innere Gleichgewicht findet sich nicht von einer Stunde zur anderen, sondern es ist der ausgezahlte Preis langen Suchens und Tastens. Ein Weg, mit Irrtümern und Fehlgriffen besät, liegt hinter einem Menschenwesen in Harmonie und echtem Frieden. Aber das Wagnis lohnt! Nur in diesem geistigen Abenteuer wird der Mensch die Wahrheit seines eigenen Wesens erkennen und sich schließlich als wahrer Mensch vollenden können. Dieser abenteuerliche Weg hat einen Namen:

Spirituelles Leben

Und das Gleichgewicht, das zwischen einer ausschließlichen Liebe zu Gott und einer ausschließlichen Liebe zu den Geschöpfen gesucht und gefunden wird, hat auch einen Namen:

Christlicher Humanismus

Der christliche Humanismus versöhnt diese beiden Pole miteinander, die scheinbar unerbittlich voneinander Abstand halten – Gott und Welt, Himmel und Erde, Schöpfer und Geschöpf: Der christliche Humanismus besteht in einer so intensiven Liebe zu Gott, daß, er alles von ihm Geschaffene mitumarmt; und er besteht in einer so tiefen und reinen Liebe zum Geschöpf, daß sie dieses vollkommen durchdringt, um letztlich im Geschöpf die Quelle alles Geschaffenen zu berühren – Gott.

Im Gegensatz zu einer exklusiven Liebe zu Gott sprechen wir jetzt von einer inklusiven Liebe zu Gott, einer ganz neuen Liebe, die alles in sich vereint. Sie schließt nichts Existierendes aus, sondern heißt es von Herzen willkommen, um es in die große Einheit hineinzunehmen und zu vergöttlichen. Sie weist nichts Menschliches zurück, sondern sie integriert es und zieht es in einer emporschwingenden Bewegung mit sich fort, dem Ziel entgegen – dem Unendlichen.

In einer solchen Liebe wird Gott unendlich geliebt und desgleichen seine Geschöpfe, auch sie werden im ganz wahren Sinn unendlich in Gott geliebt, der ja in ihnen wohnt.

Wir sagten, diese Haltung glückt nicht im ersten Augenblick, sie ist vielmehr das Ziel, das Ende und die Krönung einer Bewegung, und sie kann deshalb dialektisch genannt werden. Sie setzt das Überschreiten der beiden ersten „Ziele", die wir nannten, voraus, den Engel und das Tier. Man entkommt der Doppelversuchung, der materiellen wie der geistigen, nur, wenn man persönlich diese Erfahrung im Leben gemacht hat. So oder so muß man vom Fruchtfleisch dieser Erde gekostet haben, man muß getanzt haben nach ihrer Melodie, und man muß die Lippen am Kelch gehabt haben, um zu wissen, was die Materie in ihrer Dichte und Wirklichkeit bedeuten kann. Und weiter: Man muß in einer großen Umkehrbewegung zu Gott hin auf alle diese irdischen Freuden verzichtet haben, auf alle menschlichen Wünsche und Bedürfnisse, selbst auf die ganz natürlichen und selbstverständlichen, um in seiner Brust zu erleben, was es heißt, seinen Gott über alles zu lieben.

Erst dann tritt zu dieser Doppelerfahrung noch eine dritte hinzu, die das Gleichgewicht unserer beiden Lieben zu Schöpfer und Geschöpf wiederherstellt und garantiert, es ist die Haltung des christlichen Humanismus.

Der christliche Humanismus stellt einen VIA MEDIA dar, der keinesfalls ein Kompromiß ist, sondern die Verbindung und Synthese des Engels und des Tieres. Er überschreitet in einer doppelten Bewegung von Integration und Verneinung das eine wie das andere, um beides miteinander zu verschmelzen zu einer schlichten und einzigen Liebe.

Original:
Humanisme chrétien
(Pomfret, Connecticut/USA 1966)

Was ist eine Offenbarung?

Die religiöse Offenbarung erlaubt dem Menschen, bewußt das zu wählen, was er im Innersten und Wesentlichsten bereits ist. Sie entdeckt ihm auf der Ebene des „logos", was er auf der Seinsebene schon ist. Sie fordert ihn auf, dieses Sein jetzt frei und bewußt zu bejahen.

Seine Zustimmung, sein Eingeständnis mittels des Glaubens, ist nichts anderes als eine „Unterzeichnung" dessen, was der Mensch in seinem Herzen schon vollzogen hatte und ständig neu vollzieht. Es bedeutet seine höchste Würde, eine Würde jenseits weltlicher Begriffe und Wertschätzung, und es ist das Mysterium seines vollkommenen Entfaltens und Reifens. Sein JA, das er jetzt gibt, ist für ihn der letzte Schritt zur vollen Menschwerdung, es ist seine frei-bewußte Selbstbestätigung in seiner tiefsten und persönlichsten Wesenszone. Daher befreit der Glaube. Daher rettet der Glaube.

Man sagt, Gnade und Glaube bestünden in der Einheit. Doch wenn die Gnade Leben ist, dann darf sie nicht als eine Art biologischen Stromes gedacht werden, der durch uns hindurchgeht, ob wir es wollen oder nicht, und der uns belebt, ob wir es wissen oder nicht. Nein, die Gnade drängt sich niemandem auf, denn ihre Haupteigenschaft und Funktion ist, persönlich zu sein, ganz persönlich, und das heißt frei und bewußt, indem sie mit unserer Zustimmung arbeitet oder unsere Verweigerung gegen sie akzeptiert. Hier, an diesem Punkt, liegt alle Würde des Menschen – und zugleich sein Risiko.

Die Gnade wird uns angeboten und nicht aufgezwungen. Niemals und in keinem Fall wird sie uns bedrängen, da sie das Bewegungsfeld der frei-persönlichen und geheimen Beziehung einer Menschenseele mit ihrem Schöpfer ist. Die Gnade ist keine Wesenheit, die blind auf uns einwirkt, sondern grundsätzlich ist sie an die Qualität unserer persönlichen Beziehung mit Gott gebunden. Ihr Wirken hängt ab von der Tiefe und Intensität dieser Beziehung. Sie bedingt diese Beziehung und wird zugleich von ihr bedingt. Es besteht ein Austausch, und die Gnade selbst ist dieser Austausch. Sie ist die Ursache des Erblühens und Reifens einer Gott-menschlichen Beziehung.

Daher ist die Gnade Geist. Die Rolle des Geistes im Innern der Dreifaltigkeit besteht darin, diesen Austausch zu schaffen. Der Geist ist dieser ewig fließende und ewig persönliche Strom zwischen Vater und Sohn und zwischen Sohn und Vater, indem er die beiden vereinigt. Diese Rolle spielt der Geist auch im Herzen des Menschen, und er entspricht einem Gnadenwirken.

Das Ereignis der Offenbarung im Leben eines Menschen ist der Schritt vom unbewußten zum bewußten Glauben, vom uneingestandenen zum eingestandenen Glauben, vom verhaltenen zum offenen und bejahten Glauben. So schafft die Offenbarung nichts wesentlich Neues im Menschen und fügt auch nichts hinzu, das nicht schon da wäre und in ihm lebte. Die Offenbarung macht offen-bar, sie ent-deckt, sie ent-schleiert das Verborgene. Durch sie manifestiert sich etwas, das bislang nur versteckt lebte oder durch anderes verschüttet lag.

Was ist nun aber eine persönliche Offenbarung Gottes? Wie geschieht sie? Ist sie dem Menschen gegenüber überhaupt möglich? Und die weitere Frage: Ist eine Offenbarung Gottes dem Menschen gegenüber denn etwas Reales? Und kann sie jemals für die anderen glaubwürdig werden?

Der denkende Mensch kann durchaus auf philosophische Weise Schritt für Schritt zu einem Schöpfergott gelangen, den er dann unendlich und zugleich persönlich nennt. Soweit mag er vordringen. Doch hier muß er wohl notgedrungen stehenbleiben, denn eine innige Vertrautheit mit diesem verstandesmäßig gefundenen Gott bleibt dem philosophisch Denkenden verschlossen. Er würde sogar seinen Glauben schrittweise wieder einschränken, wenn Gott jetzt nicht die Initiative ergriffe und sich dem suchenden Menschen offenbarte.

Da wir bereits von einem persönlichen Gott ausgehen, ist es demnach nicht unsinnig, sich diesen Gott auch persönlich handelnd vorzustellen, indem er mit jenem anderen Geistwesen, dem Menschen, Beziehung aufnimmt. Wer wollte diese Möglichkeit von vornherein bestreiten und mit welchem Argument?

Da die Schöpfung ein freies Werk der Liebe ist und Gott keinerlei Zwang unterliegt – das stünde im Widerspruch zum Prinzip der göttlichen Freiheit –, so ist es nicht unlogisch, sich vorzustellen, daß Gott auch einen Dialog mit dem Menschen beginnt, den er erschuf „nach seinem Bild und Gleichnis". Gott spricht zu diesem Menschen. Die gesamte Schöpfung ist eine Liebeshandlung, und ein solcher Gesprächsbeginn zwischen Schöpfer und Geschöpf gilt als eine Schöpfungsverlängerung. Im Zusammenhang aller Schöpfungsaspekte, die auf Geben und Empfangen beruhen, erscheint das durchaus verständlich.

Zu dieser Offenbarungsbegründung, die das lebendige Gotteswesen als Quelle begreift, kommt die andere, die den Menschen als Empfänger betrifft: Tatsächlich ist die Natur des Menschen, indem sie die Fähigkeit in sich trägt, im Unendlichen aufzugehen (sogar als eine Forderung von seiten Gottes!), so beschaffen, daß eine Selbstoffenbarung Gottes vorstellbar ist, damit der Mensch sich ihm verbinde und die Liebe beiderseitig werde ...

Dieser Zielpunkt des Menschen, Gott, kann durch eine blinde, unbewußte und gleichsam mechanische Lebensweise, auf dem Niveau von Pflanze und Tier, nicht erreicht werden. Gott, Endziel des Menschen, ist ein persönliches Wesen und kann daher nur in einem frei-persönlichen Akt erreicht werden, ganz frei und voll bewußt. Das aber setzt ein „Sichtbarwerden" dieses Zieles voraus, also ein Offenbarwerden Gottes.

Wir sehen, daß sich Gottes Offenbarungsmöglichkeit in unser forschendes Denken als notwendig eingliedert, ganz der Natur des Menschen und seiner ontologischen Forderung durch Gott entsprechend. Ohne sie bliebe alle Sehnsucht des Menschen eine Zielsuche ohne Ende. Diese Sehnsucht kann sich nicht im Leeren verlieren, oder alles wäre absurd. Und demjenigen, der uns vorwirft, die souveräne Freiheit Gottes damit zu verletzen, muß geantwortet werden: Der Schöpfer selbst hat ins Herz des Menschen einen göttlichen Anspruch gepflanzt, und wenn er ihm diesen erfüllen will, dann nur in eben dieser souveränen Freiheit. Gott handelt hier notwendig und zugleich in seiner vollkommenen Freiheit (vgl. Henri de Lubac: „Das Übernatürliche", Schlußfolgerung).

Soweit über die Möglichkeit einer Offenbarung. Nun gilt es, auf die Frage einzugehen, ob eine solche Offenbarung etwas Reales ist und als etwas Reales glaubwürdig weitergegeben werden kann.

Wir kommen nur weiter, wenn wir zunächst die Geschichte befragen, denn sie zeigt uns eine religiöse Glaubenspraxis seit den Zeiten primitivster menschlicher Zivilisation. Von Religion im strengen Sinn dürfen wir jedoch erst dann sprechen, wenn es sich nicht nur um das Bemühen des Menschen handelt, mit Gott Beziehung aufzunehmen, sondern wenn wir eine tatsächliche Antwort Gottes an den Menschen beobachten können. An diesem Punkt sind die großen Weltreligionen entstanden. Alle behaupten sie, aus einer direkten Gottesoffenbarung an ihre Propheten geboren zu sein.

Der Prophet ist ein Mensch, zu dem Gott spricht; und der Prophet ist derjenige, der im Namen Gottes zu den Menschen spricht. Mit anderen Worten, es genügt nicht, daß Gott sich persönlich an einen Menschen wendet und sich ihm in einem besonderen Offenbarungsgeschehen verständlich macht, damit dieses Wesen fortan „Prophet" genannt werden kann. Zugleich muß dieser Mensch seine Mission verstehen, diese göttliche Offenbarung den anderen Menschen zu vermitteln. Alle, die an seine Botschaft glauben werden, nennen sich dann die Adepten dieser neuen Religion, als deren Begründer der Prophet gilt. Nach seinem Tode wird seine Lehre schriftlich festgehalten, um Irrtümer bei der Weitergabe zu vermeiden. So entsteht eine Heilige Schrift.

Worin liegt der Wert dieses neuen, heiligen Buches? Er liegt allein in der Offenbarung als sein Ursprung, seine Quelle. Natürlich geht es hier nicht um eine Kontrolle der Echtheit und Glaubwürdigkeit des objektiv wahren Charakters einer Offenbarung, so wie man den Wahrheitsgehalt einer Kopie untersucht, indem man sie mit ihrem Original vergleicht. Im Fall einer Offenbarung ist das Original Gott und scheidet daher als Vergleichsobjekt aus.

Der Prophet, alleiniger Zeuge dieses einzigartigen Ereignisses einer speziellen Offenbarung Gottes, kann keine begrifflichen Beweisstücke über das liefern, was er sagt, als einzig die Kraft und die Stärke seiner Aussage sowie seines persönlichen Zeugnisses als Mensch. Von einer Beweisforderung über die Echtheit der Offenbarung im objektiv-wissenschaftlichen Sinn des Wortes ist also abzulassen, weil sie nicht möglich ist.

Müssen wir demnach einer Verstandesrechtfertigung der Religion entsagen? Nein, denn wir haben Kriterien der Echtheit, die dem Verstand erlauben, sich zu äußern und zu urteilen:

Der Prophet, sagten wir, hat nicht mehr vorzulegen als sein persönliches Zeugnis. Ist ein solcher Fall aber so einzigartig in unserer menschlichen Welt? Wie viel haben wir schon von anderen gehört und arglos übernommen! Unser hauptsächliches Wissen gründen wir auf den Glauben einer fremden Zeugenschaft, und wir denken nicht daran, diesen Zeugen als Betrüger abzutun. Die Erfahrung sagt uns: Wenn der Zeuge zuverlässig, wahrhaftig und menschlich vertrauenerweckend erscheint, dann haben wir keinen Grund anzunehmen, er wolle uns betrügen. Es ist unsererseits normal und vernünftig, ihm zu glauben – andernfalls wäre unser Leben auf allen Ebenen unlebbar.

Der Glaube an eine Zeugenschaft ist demnach nichts Irrationales oder Zweifelhaftes. Vielmehr vollzieht er sich im Einklang mit unserer menschlichen Natur und innerhalb der Ordnung aller Dinge. Doch muß, damit einer Zeugenaussage geglaubt wird – vor allem wenn es sich um eine derart bedeutende und außergewöhnliche Tatsache einer göttlichen Offenbarung handelt –, diese Offenbarung von einer gewissen Anzahl von Echtheitskriterien begleitet sein. Es sind die Prüfsteine, die unserem Glauben einen rationalen oder wenigstens vernünftigen Charakter geben.

Welches sind die Wertmesser der Echtheit?

Der erste und wichtigste ist der menschliche Wert des Zeugen. Wenn diese Person ehrlich, fest, gradlinig, psychisch gesund und ausgeglichen ist, dann hat sie gute Aussichten, daß ihr Angebot angenommen wird. Wenn dieser Zeuge ferner bereit ist, für seine Wahrheit zu leiden – und er bringt sich innerlich bereits um, indem er seine Botschaft gegen Spötter und Leugner verteidigt –, dann ist es nicht nur vernünftig, dieser Wahrheit Glauben zu schenken, sondern es wäre geradezu unklug, ihr unseren Glauben zu verweigern.

Wenn aber unser Prophet nicht zum Äußersten bereit ist, d. h. selbst durch sein Sterben Zeugnis abzulegen für die Lauterkeit seiner Person und die Wahrheit seiner Aussage, dann könnte man noch immer ein verstecktes persönliches Interesse, einen heimlichen Ehrgeiz hinter allem vermuten. Stirbt er aber, um sein Zeugnis mit seinem Leben zu besiegeln, das er nur einmal zu geben vermag, dann beweist er in entwaffnender Form sein Desinteresse hinsichtlich seiner Person, und damit wird die Echtheit seiner Botschaft offenkundig.

Paulus erwiderte: „Warum weint Ihr und macht mir das Herz schwer? Ich bin bereit, mich nicht allein fesseln zu lassen, vielmehr auch in Jerusalem zu sterben für den Namen des Herrn Jesus."

(Apostelgeschichte 21, 13)

Der Märtyrer wird somit unbestritten zum wahrhaftigsten und zuverlässigsten Zeugen, zum Zeugen par excellence. Wenn in Offenbarungstexten von übernatürlichen Ereignissen und Wundern die Rede ist, durch die Gott dem heiligen Charakter der Mission seines Propheten „Gesetzeskraft" gibt, dann wäre es töricht, an seinem Zeugnis zu zweifeln.

Alle diese Kriterien betreffen die Person des Zeugen; hinzu kommt aber nun der Inhalt der Botschaft! Dieser sollte dem menschlich-moralischen Denken und Fühlen nicht zuwiderlaufen. Die Botschaft einer Offenbarung sollte wirklich von moralischem und religiösem Gehalt sein, aufbauend für jene, die sie hören werden. Wenn auch diese letzte Bedingung erfüllt ist, dann haben wir alles beisammen, um vernünftig glauben zu können.

Jetzt können wir uns einen Begriff davon machen, wie sich der Glaube vor dem Tribunal des Verstandes zu rechtfertigen weiß und auf welche Weise die Wahrheit einer Religion beurteilt wird. Legen wir diese Wertmesser an die Religionen an, die wir kennen, dann scheint uns das Christentum in ganz wunderbarer Weise aus dem Ensemble aller Religionen emporzusteigen. Wir werden an einen Punkt geführt, an dem wir das Christentum als die wirklich ganz und gar authentische Religion erkennen und ihrer Schrift einen wahrhaft heiligen Charakter zusprechen.

Doch ist das Christentum mehr noch als eine Offenbarung: Es ist eine Gotteshandlung, eine Umwandlung! Es ist Schöpfung, eine Neuschöpfung! Christus war nicht nur daran gelegen, uns zu lehren, was der Mensch in Wahrheit sei, sondern er war gekommen, um den Menschen zu verändern, umzuschaffen und zu retten.

Demnach offenbart das Christentum einen Doppelaspekt: Den Aspekt des Glaubens und der Erkenntnisoffenbarung einerseits, und den Aspekt der göttlichen Gnade, des Lebens und der Erlösung andererseits. Das Christentum ist der Dialog dieser beiden Aspekte, es ist die Dialektik zwischen dem einen und dem anderen, es ist das Wachstum des einen durch das andere.

Original:
Révélation et Grâce (Kairo/Ägypten 1960) und
Révélation (Beirut/Libanon 1962)

Über die Glaubwürdigkeit einer Zeugenaussage

Wer kennt den historischen Jesus?

In unseren Tagen setzt man häufig den Jesus des reinen Glaubens – nur er scheint dem menschlichen Geist zugänglich – einem Jesus der Geschichte gegenüber, der dazu verurteilt ist, der große Unbekannte für uns zu bleiben. Die Argumente, die man einbringt, wirken solide.

Es ist wahr, wir kennen Jesus nur aus den Evangelien, die das Werk seiner gläubigen Jünger sind, der Propagandisten des Christentums. Die drei ersten Evangelien, mehr als dreißig Jahre nach dem Tod ihres Meisters verfaßt, sind mit Vorurteilen der Urkirche durchsetzt, die Kritik hat uns das deutlich geziegt. Hielten wir uns allein an sie, dann hätten wir vielmehr historische Dokumente über die Glaubensweise der ersten Christen als über die Christusperson selbst.

Das Johannesevangelium dagegen, erst gegen Ende des ersten Jahrhunderts niedergeschrieben, ist vor allem eine mystische Kontemplation über einen idealen Logos, der aus dieser Sicht keinerlei Verbindung mit dem historischen Jesus von Nazareth haben muß. Was soll man sagen? Wir können nichts sagen, bevor wir nicht unseren Wortbegriff „Geschichte" klargestellt haben. Was ist Geschichte?

Die Geschichte ist ein Versuch, menschliche Ereignisse aufgrund einer Dokumentation verständlich zu machen. Die ersten Schritte, die der Historiker unternimmt, sind Zusammentragung von Zeugnissen und ihre Wertprüfung. Wenn dies getan ist, wird er sein persönliches Urteil über diese Dokumentation fällen. In seinem Urteil müssen zunächst die Ereignisse in ihrer objektiven Wirklichkeit rekonstruiert werden, dann muß der Historiker diese Ereignisse erklären, d. h. er muß sie verständlich machen, er muß ihren Sinn deuten, ihre Bedeutung finden.

All das betrifft das Problem einer materiellen Rekonstruktion von Tatsachen, das sich bei der Gegenüberstellung von Zeugnissen und Kritik ergibt. Kommen wir aber zum Problem der Deutung und Sinnfindung, dem letzten Ziel aller Geschichtsschreibung. Was heißt, eine geschichtliche Tatsache deuten?

Ein natürliches, physisches Geschehen erklärt sich durch natürliche und physische Ursachen. Die Objektivität, in der man an diese Sache herangeht, besteht darin, sich auf einem materiell-fühlbaren, sinnlich-wahrnehmbaren Feld zu bewegen. Doch ein geschichtliches Geschehen war in Wirklichkeit kein physisches Geschehen, sondern ein rein menschliches! Also fordert es als Verständlichkeitsprinzip eine Ursache metaphysischer und geistiger Ordnung; der Mensch als geistiger Urheber steht hinter allem Geschehen. In dem Maß, in dem der Historiker also gewillt ist, das Terrain einer physischen Rekonstruktion zu überwinden, um eine wahre Interpretation des Ereignisses zu finden, tritt er in den Bereich des Metaphysischen und Spirituellen.

Nun wird es sich zeigen, daß die Interpretation, die wir vom Historiker erhalten, dem Wert seines philosophischen Denkens entspricht. Seine Art zu denken und zu forschen, mit der er jetzt die tieferen Beweggründe der Menschen jenseits und mittels ihres Handelns zu entschlüsseln und uns zu erklären sucht, entspricht der geistigen Klarheit seines Blickes und seiner persönlichen Erfahrung im Bereich des Menschlichen. Mit einem Wort, der Wert des Historikers bestimmt letztlich den Wert seiner Geschichtsschreibung. Die Qualität seiner Interpretation hängt ab von der Qualität seiner menschlichen und spirituellen Erfahrung.

Demnach wird die Geschichte nicht festgehalten wie von einer Kamera, sondern sie wird aufgenommen, verarbeitet und weitergegeben von einem menschlichen Herzen, vom Geist und ganzen Wesen des Historikers und dessen praktischer Lebenserfahrung.

Wir sehen hier, bis zu welchem Grad die persönliche Qualität des Historikers bei jeder Art von Geschichtsschreibung ausschlaggebend ist und das bereits bei der Auswahl und im Urteil über die zur Verfügung stehenden Zeugnisse, später in der Interpretationsweise des Geschehens. Auf den Einwand, dies sei Subjektivismus, muß man antworten: Sobald man den Bereich der Naturwissenschaften verläßt, verliert der Gegensatz zwischen Objektivität und Subjektivität an Bedeutung, er sagt uns nicht mehr viel, denn wir erkennen, daß sich die Verständlichkeit eines Geschehens vielmehr im Geschehen selbst offenbart als in der Empfindung des Historikers, der es uns deuten wird.

Ein Beispiel: Die beste Rekonstruktion eines Kriminalfalls soll nicht im Verbalprozeß des Untersuchungsrichters gesehen werden, so vollständig und präzise dieser auch verlaufen mag, sondern in der Bewußtseinstiefe des Mörders, im komplexen Spiel seiner heimlichen Handlungtendenzen und tiefen Absichten. Dieses Herz muß gelesen werden! Dort findet sich die Erklärung, nur dort kann sie überhaupt gefunden werden, und dann wird sie das Schlußwort eines intensiven Bemühens und Verstehenwollens sein, eines menschlichen Entgegenkommens, einer Kommunion.

Das wiederum wird nur dem vetrauten Freund möglich sein, dessen Blick klar geworden ist in Freundschaft und Zuneigung, nur er kann tatsächlich die Motive des verübten Aktes begreifen, weil er einzudringen vermag in die Seele des Angeklagten. Er allein könnte die wahre Geschichte dieses Verbrechens beschreiben, denn nur er ist imstande, die volle Wahrheit zu erfassen und sie uns mitzuteilen.

So unterscheiden wir zwei Arten von Zeugen:

Einmal gibt es den „fremden Zeugen", der zufällig beim Geschehen anwesend war. Dieser ist in der Lage, das Ereignis gut und detailliert zu beschreiben. Dann gibt es den „nahestehenden Zeugen", der die Person des Täters wirklich kennt. Dieser zweite ist in der Lage, das Drama in seiner Gesamtheit wirklich zu verstehen und es uns in seinen wahren Zusammenhängen, Hintergründen und Motiven zu erklären, selbst dann, wenn er persönlich am Tatort nicht anwesend war!

Sagt man jetzt, daß der zweite Zeuge nicht den Namen „Zeuge" verdient, allenfalls im übertragenen Sinn? ... Nein, der eine wie der andere sind authentische Zeugen des Verbrechens, jeder auf seiner

Ebene. Der erste ist es in äußerer Hinsicht, der zweite in innerer. Und dieser zweite ist nicht weniger objektiv als der erste. Der eine hat die Szene mit eigenen Augen erlebt und bezeugt somit klar und deutlich das Gesehene, ohne daß er es verstehen und seine Zeugenaussage inhaltlich rechtfertigen könnte, denn ein Zeuge erweist sich nicht als Wissender, er bestätigt eher sich selbst, er stellt sich als Beobachter eines Geschehens dar. Auch der andere „hat gesehen", doch nicht den äußeren Ablauf des Geschehens, sondern den inneren, eine andere Wirklichkeit, die er als Zeuge am Tatort nicht besser beweisen und rechtfertigen könnte, denn auch hier beweist die Zeugenaussage sich nicht selbst. Folglich haben wir es in beiden Fällen mit einem „Beweis" zu tun, mit dem fühlbaren, äußeren Beweis in dem ersten Zeugenfall und mit dem persönlichen, inneren Beweis im zweiten Zeugenfall. Dieser zweite aber erst bringt Sicherheit, er schafft das Fundament der Zeugenschaft, verleiht ihr Kraft und Aussage.

Wird man nun sagen, daß die erste Art einer Zeugenaussage zuverlässiger und glaubwürdiger ist, da besser nachprüfbar und vergleichbar mit allem zur Verfügung stehenden Material? Nein, denn eine ähnliche Nachprüfung kann ebensogut auch in jener zweiten Zeugenart durchgeführt werden und zwar durch Zeugenvernehmung und Vergleiche der Aussagen aller Personen, die den Urheber des Dramas persönlich gekannt haben.

All das zeigt uns gut, daß die innere, geistige Zeugenschaft keinen geringeren Wert besitzt als die äußere, physische. Sie besitzt sogar einen höheren, denn der aufklärende und ausdeutende Aspekt wird den Sieg über den rein beschreibenden Aspekt davontragen.

Ein Letztes gibt es zum Begriff der Geschichte zu untersuchen, und das ist der Zeitfaktor. Im allgemeinen glaubt man, daß unsere Beziehung zu einem Erlebnis und dessen Darstellung durch die Jahre, die dazwischentreten, verfälscht werden. Nach einer gewissen Zeit wird die Wahrheit unbestimmbar sein. Wenn das richtig ist im Fall der äußeren und beschreibenden Zeugenschaft, so gilt das keinesfalls für die innere und ausdeutende Zeugenschaft! In diesem zweiten Fall geschieht sogar das Gegenteil: Die verstrichene Zeit wird zum zusätzlichen Garanten für die Tiefe und Klarheit der Betrachtung. In Wirklichkeit erkennt man den Wert eines Ereignisses besser nach einigen Jahrzehnten Distanz als im Augenblick oder schon sehr bald danach. Den europäischen Ländern fällt es heute viel leichter, Leben und Bedeutung von Napoleon, Maria Theresia oder Friedrich II. zu beurteilen und niederzuschreiben, d.h. es geschichtlich zu deuten, als dasselbe über einen ihrer Zeitgenossen zu tun.

Doch um nicht in die Ferne zu schweifen, haben wir nicht selbst auf unserer Lebensstrecke schon diese Erfahrung gemacht? Dieses oder jenes harmlose Erlebnis, das wir wegen seiner scheinbaren Nichtigkeit nicht einmal in einem persönlichen Tagebuch festgehalten haben, gewinnt nach zehn, zwanzig oder dreißig Jahren Abstand plötzlich in ganz außergewöhnlicher Weise Profil. Jetzt erkennen wir, daß diese Stunde unter Umständen ein Markstein oder sogar ein Wendepunkt unserer Lebensgeschichte war.

All das zeigt, daß in der Geschichtsbetrachtung der Zeitfaktor wesentlich ist, und daß dieser keineswegs der Objektivität einer Interpretation im Wege steht und unsere Sicht verhindert. Im Gegenteil, die dazwischenliegende Zeit ist von Vorteil.

Ich versuche nun, all das bisher Gesagte auf das Problem des historischen Jesus von Nazareth anzuwenden und dabei auf verständliche Einwände zu antworten, die ich deshalb bereits erwähnt hatte.

Die Evangelien sind die Werke der gläubigen Jünger Jesu. Müssen sie uns deshalb „verdächtig" erscheinen? Ich denke nicht, im Gegenteil! Ich glaube, daß die Apostel befähigter waren als jeder andere, das wahre Porträt Jesu zu zeichnen. Fast ununterbrochen haben sie als engste Freunde drei Jahre in der vertrauten Nähe des Meisters gelebt, sie sind mit ihm mitgegangen und haben viel Freude und Erschütterung mit ihm geteilt. So waren sie die einzigen Zeitgenossen Jesu, die auch inner-menschlich verstanden haben und demnach eine äußere und innere Zeugenaussage machen können, beides! Sie sind ganz gewiß in der Lage, uns einen guten Bericht zu geben und uns das Erlebte auch zu deuten.

Was ich hier von den Aposteln im allgemeinen behaupte, das muß ich ganz im besonderen von Johannes sagen. Johannes, der Jünger, den Jesus liebte und der in der letzten gemeinsamen Stunde an Jesu Brust geruht hat, ist wohl auch derjenige, der am tiefsten in Jesu Wesen eingedrungen ist und der es uns deshalb am vollkommensten wiedergeben kann. Diese sehr besondere Freundschaft, die ihn mit Jesus verband, erlaubte ihm, in Jesus Dimensionen zu entdecken, die von den anderen Jüngern kaum erahnt werden konnten, geschweige denn dargestellt. Denn die Liebe läßt uns keinesfalls erblinden, wie es das Sprichwort will, sondern die Liebe ist gerade die einzige Quelle der Klarheit, die wir haben können, um unsere Mitmenschen in ihrer Tiefe zu erfassen und ganz zu verstehen.

Leider bezeichnet man deshalb das Johannes-Evangelium gewöhnlich als das am wenigsten historische der vier. Für mich persönlich ist es jedoch das historischste, weil es von der Liebe geschrieben wurde, die allein versteht. Durch sie wurde Christus in seiner tiefsten Wirklichkeit und Weite erkannt. Hören wir aus dem Johannes-Prolog:

> *Im Anfang war das Wort, und das Wort war bei Gott, und Gott war das Wort. Dieses war im Anfang bei Gott; und alles ist durch es geworden, nichts von dem, was geworden ist, ward ohne dieses. In ihm war Leben, und das Leben war das Licht der Menschen. Das Licht leuchtet in der Finsternis, und die Finsternis hat es nicht begriffen.*
>
> ...
>
> *Da kam das wahre Licht, das jeden Menschen erleuchtet, in diese Welt. Er war in der Welt, die Welt ist ja durch Ihn gemacht, und doch hat die Welt Ihn nicht erkannt. Er kam in Sein Eigentum, die Seinen aber nahmen ihn nicht auf. Doch allen, die Ihn aufnahmen, verlieh er Kraft, Kinder Gottes zu werden.*
>
> ...
>
> *Und das Wort ist Fleisch geworden und hat unter uns gewohnt. Wir haben Seine Herrlichkeit gesehen, eine Herrlichkeit wie die eines Eingeborenen vom Vater, voll Gnade und Wahrheit ... Aus Seiner Fülle haben wir alle empfangen, Gnade um Gnade.*

(Johannes 1)

Neben dem Argument „Liebe" gibt es noch das Argument „Zeit", nachdem das Johannes-Evangelium historischer zu nennen ist als die anderen drei, denn es ist lange nach den drei anderen verfaßt worden. Mehr als sechzig Jahre der Reflexion und der Meditation haben Johannes erlaubt, anhand der Werke und Worte Jesu das Wesentlichste der Christusperson und seiner Weltbotschaft zu entwickeln. Daher ist dieses Evangelium für uns das reifste und das apostolischste Zeugnis, das wir über Jesus besitzen. Der Zeitfaktor spielte hier seine begünstigende Rolle für die Treue und Authentizität der Zeugenaussage.

Was ich über Johannes sagte, könnte ich auf die gesamte Erfahrung der Urkirche ausdehnen und auf die Kirche im allgemeinen. Die grundlegenden Züge Christi und des Christentums haben sich erst „mit der Zeit" mehr und mehr entfalten können, und das ist normal.

Nun reichen aber die Feststellungen, die für jede Geschichtsschreibung und jedes Geschichtsverständnis gelten, keinesfalls für das Phänomen des Christentums aus. Die fortschreitende Entwicklung der Darstellung der Christusperson innerhalb der christlichen Lehre ist nichts anderes als unsere menschliche und geistige Entdeckungsreise, und sie wird Interpretationsfehlern immer ausgesetzt bleiben – Teilbestand eines jeden Erkenntniswissens. Die christliche Lehre aber besitzt ihre eigene Garantie der Echtheit, die ihr erlaubt, die Wahrheit von Irrtum und Irrlehre zu unterscheiden. Dieses in ihr waltende und wachende Prinzip ist der Heilige Geist, der die Kirche bewohnt und der bei aller Interpretationsarbeit anwesend ist, mithandelnd anwesend!

Ich will den Vater bitten, und Er wird euch
einen anderen Beistand verleihen, damit Er
in Ewigkeit bei euch bleibe. Den Geist der
Wahrheit ... Er bleibt bei euch und wird in
euch sein. Ich lasse euch nicht als Waisen
zurück. Ich komme zu euch ... Der Heilige Geist,
der Beistand, den der Vater in Meinem Namen
senden wird, wird euch alles lehren und euch
an alles erinnern, was Ich euch gesagt habe.

(aus den Abschiedsreden Jesu, Johannes 14)

Gott hat es durch den Geist uns geoffenbart; der Geist ergründet nämlich alles, selbst die Tiefen der Gottheit. Wer von den Menschen kennt das Wesen des Menschen, außer der Geist des Menschen, der in seinem Innern ist? Und so erkennt auch niemand das Wesen Gottes, außer der Geist Gottes.

(Paulus an die Korinther I, 2, 10-11)

So ist der Geist des lebendigen Christus in der Kirche das letzte, höchste und entscheidende Kriterium für alles Unterscheiden und Erkennen. Ein näheres Eingehen auf dieses Thema ist an dieser Stelle nicht möglich.

Wenn man wollte, könnte man also von einem „Christus des Glaubens" sprechen, aber unter der Bedingung, sofort klarzustellen, daß der „Christus der Geschichte" gemeint ist, Jesus von Nazareth, und kein anderer. Ein Christus, der heute besser denn je gekannt, verstanden und dargestellt wird. Der Glaube ist ja nicht, wie vielfach angenommen wird, eine abstrakte Betrachtung von unsichtbaren, unerreichbaren, also übernatürlichen Wirklichkeiten, sondern wahrer Glaube ist helle Geistesklarheit und Blickschärfe, die dem gewöhnlich Sterblichen erlaubt, in der Alltagswelt unbekannte Dimensionen zu entdecken. Der Glaube erfindet nicht, sondern er schafft klare Formulierungen dessen, was bislang uneingestanden schon im Herzen erlebt worden ist. Der Glaube ent-deckt. Weit entfernt davon, eigene Schöpfung, Wunsch- oder Traumbild zu sein, ist der Glaube im Herzen des Gläubigen das Echo der tiefsten und letzten Wirklichkeit.

In diesem Sinn trifft sich der Glaube mit dem ethymologischen Sinn des Wortes „Geschichte", denn „istorein" bedeutet im Griechischen ursprünglich „nachforschen, prüfen".

Von hier aus sieht man deutlich, wie nutzlos es ist, die Christusperson des Glaubens derjenigen der Geschichte entgegenzusetzen. Die elementarste Reflexion über die „historische Methodik" genügte, um diese künstliche Unterscheidung zu zerstören. Der Christus des Glaubens ist dem der Geschichte gleichbedeutend, er ist der historische Jesus von Nazareth, den die Jünger, die Apostel und unzählbare Generationen von Christen ständig besser und besser erkannt haben und die bis zum heutigen Tage darum ringen, ihn immer noch tiefer und wahrer zu erkennen und über ihn zu berichten.

Auch die uns nachfolgenden Generationen werden damit an kein Ende kommen, denn unsere menschliche Geschichte wird nicht ausreichen, den unergründlichen Reichtum desjenigen zu begreifen, der Gottessohn ist und Mensch geworden war.

Original:
Connaîtrons-nous jamais le Jésus de l' histoire?
(Beirut/Libanon 1963)

Die Armut Gottes

Armut und Dreifaltigkeit

Um die Armut zu verstehen, muß man auf Gott zurückgehen. Die Armut hat ihre Quelle in Gott, denn Gott ist der große Arme, der Arme par excellence. Tatsächlich ist das Dreifaltigkeitsmysterium in seiner Tiefe grenzenlose Armut; es wäre nicht möglich ohne diese grundsätzliche Armut jeder der drei göttlichen Personen, die sich entäußern, um sich hinzugeben und zu empfangen.

DER VATER IST DER GROSSE ARME, denn alles, was er hat, und alles, was er ist, gibt er unaufhörlich an den Sohn, indem er sich in ihn ergießt und nichts für sich einbehält. Freilich ist Gott in gewissem Sinn der Reiche par excellence, da er Quelle und Ursprung a l l e n Seins ist und demnach auch des Sohnes. Gleichzeitig aber ist er der große Arme, da er diesen Reichtum, der in ihm ist, nicht als sein Eigentum hütet, sondern ihn vollständig einem andern zuwendet, dem er ganz gehören soll. Dieser andere ist der Sohn.

Wie die Quelle, die entspringt und verschwenderisch ihr Wasser verschenkt und niemals daran denkt, etwas für sich einzubehalten, so ergießt sich der Vater ganz und gar als ein ewiger Quellfluß in den Sohn.

DER SOHN IST DER GROSSE ARME, weil er aus sich heraus nichts besitzt und nichts ist durch sich allein. Er empfängt sich selbst aus dem Vater, ohne den Vater wäre er nichts. Der Sohn stammt vollkommen aus dem Vater und lebt aus ihm:

Er ist Gott von Gott,
Licht vom Licht,
wahrer Gott vom wahren Gott ...

(Credo)

Er ist „gezeugt, nicht geschaffen", d.h. er geht vollkommen aus einem andern hervor, und dieser andere ist Gott. Grundsätzliche Armut also, nackte Armut, die vom unendlichen Reichtum des Vaters erfüllt wird.

Das aber ist noch nicht das Ganze, denn der Sohn gibt die erhaltene Gabe zurück an den Vater. Nichts will er für sich in Anspruch nehmen und in sich einbehalten. Wie er nur Empfänger ist, so will er auch nur Geber sein; er will sich und die Gabe zurückgeben an denjenigen, der sein Ursprung ist.

DER GEIST IST DER GROSSE ARME, denn er existiert nur durch den Vater und den Sohn. Er ist dieser Quellsprudel ihrer gegenseitigen Liebe, und von dieser Liebe wird der Geist gebildet. Er ist die Gabe des einen an den andern, und er ist derjenige, der dieses Gebenwollen erweckt. In geheimnisvoller Diskretion und Unauffälligkeit bleibt der Geist im Hintergrund des trinitarischen Geschehens; er löscht sich vor den beiden anderen Personen, die er in Erscheinung treten läßt, aus.

Wenn der Geist nur durch diese beiden Personen existiert, so existiert er auch nur für sie: Er bildet ihre gegenseitige Anwesenheit füreinander, das Band, das diese erhält. Er ist reiner Mittler, der sich verzehrt im Vater und im Sohn, indem er einen in den andern einschmelzt. Aufgrund dieser essentiellen Armut wurde der Geist von der Kirche „der Vater der Armen" genannt: PATER PAUPERUM.

Armut und Schöpfung

Diese Bewegung des Gebens und Nehmens, die das Dreifaltigkeitsmysterium bildet, wird in ihrer Energie eine Welt erzeugen, viele Welten, ein Universum – das wir „Schöpfung" nennen. Die Schöpfung ist der Ausläufer der trinitarischen Aktivität aufgrund ihrer Intensität, ihrer Stärke. Wenn es das Wesen Gottes ist zu geben, sich zu geben, dann muß diese Gabe, da sie von Gott kommt, unendlich weit reichen. In diesem Sinn kann man von einer „Notwendigkeit der Schöpfung" sprechen. Und das ist wahr: Allein die Tatsache, daß es die Schöpfung gibt, ist in gewissem Sinn schon der Beweis für ihre Notwendigkeit, denn in Gott gibt es keinen Raum für Eventualitäten. Alles, was besteht, muß existieren.

Selbstverständlich muß nichts durch einen äußeren Zwang geschaffen werden, als Verpflichtung, sondern als eine innere, aber wesentliche Notwendigkeit, eine Notwendigkeit der Liebe. Die Schöpfung ist der freiste Akt, der denkbar ist, dazu „gratis", und zugleich ist er der notwendigste für Gott, denn ein Liebeswunsch wird nur gestillt in Überschwang und Überfluß.

Armut und Inkarnation

Nachdem Gott uns in der Schöpfung gibt, was er hat, wird er uns jetzt geben, was er ist – in der Inkarnation des Sohnes. Können wir denn noch mehr erwarten?

So sehr hat Gott die Welt geliebt, daß er Seinen eingeborenen Sohn hingab, damit, wer immer an Ihn glaubt, nicht verlorengehe, vielmehr ewiges Leben habe.

(Johannes 3, 16)

Entäußerung des Vaters, der seinen Sohn hingibt, Entäußerung des Sohnes, der sich selbst hingibt und die Kenose akzeptiert (Kenose = griechisch: „Entäußerung"; die Lehre, daß der Gottmensch bei der Menschwerdung auf die Ausübung seiner göttlichen Eigenschaften sowie auf ihren Besitz verzichtet habe):

Obwohl Er sich in der Gestalt Gottes befand,
wollte Er dennoch nicht gewaltsam
an seiner Gottesgleichheit festhalten,
vielmehr entäußerte Er sich,
nahm Knechtsgestalt an
und ward den Menschen ähnlich.

(Paulus an die Philipper II, 6-7a)

Und das WORT ist Fleisch geworden
und hat unter uns gewohnt.

(Johannes 1, 14a)

Wir sind daran gewöhnt, die Armut von Bethlehem als den Gipfel äußerster Armut anzusehen, aber die Armut von Bethlehem ist nichts im Vergleich zur Armut der Inkarnation selbst, sie ist ein Widerschein, ein Symbol nur, eine äußere Manifestation. Die wahre, sich vollständig entblätternde Armut bedeutet für Gott seinen „Abstieg" ins Fleisch.

Obgleich Er reich war, ward Er euretwegen arm,
damit ihr durch Seine Armut reich würdet.

(II Korinther 8, 9)

In der Kenose der Inkarnation zeigt sich wahrhaft die Armut Gottes. Alles, was dann folgt – die Geburt im Stall, die Flucht nach Ägypten, die Arbeit in der Schreinerwerkstatt in Nazareth, die erschöpfenden Wanderungen auf den Straßen Palästinas, *„nicht einmal einen Stein besitzend, um das Haupt darauf auszuruhen"* – ist einfaches Beiwerk in Beziehung zur grundsätzlichen Armut unseres Gottes, der Mensch geworden war.

Armut und Erlösung

Hier sind wir am Höhepunkt göttlicher Armut, am Gipfel, der eher ein Abgrund ist, ein Wahnsinn, ein Un-Sinn. Aber Romano Guardini sagt:

Die Liebe tut solche Dinge.

So wie er seine Göttlichkeit bei der Inkarnation abgestreift hatte, so wird er bei der Erlösung selbst sein Menschsein von sich streifen.

Wie viele seinetwegen sich entsetzten, so sehr
entstellt war Er, so wenig sah Er andern Menschen
ähnlich, so wenig andern Menschenkindern gleich.
...
Er ist verachtet und von aller Welt verlassen,
ein Schmerzensmann, dem Leiden wohlbekannt,
verachtet so wie einer, der sein Angesicht vor uns
verhüllen muß.

(Heilsverkündung des Propheten Isaias 52, 14. 53, 3)

Für den Menschen ist das wertvollste Gut nicht sein Leben, sondern seine Ehre. Der Mensch ist fähig, freiwillig sein Leben hinzugeben, um seine Ehre zu retten – und wir erleben das häufig. Jesu Passion aber führte bis zum Verlust von Leib und Ehre. Sein Leben hinzugeben bedeutete in gewissem Maß nichts für ihn, schrecklich aber war es, seinAnsehen zu opfern, zum Gespött des Volkes zu werden, dessen „König" er gewesen war, dessen Gott und alle Hoffnung und Erwartung.

Man kann vom Kreuz dasselbe sagen, was wir von der nackten Armut Bethlehems gesagt hatten. Die Nacktheit des Kreuzes ist nur das Symbol einer viel weiterreichenden und tiefergehenden Entblößung, es ist die grundsätzliche A r m u t Gottes, unendliche Male schrecklicher, die Jesus am Kreuz aufschreien läßt:

ELOI, ELOI, LAMA SABACHTHANI!

Mein Gott, mein Gott,
warum hast Du Mich verlassen?

(Markus 15, 34)

Original
La pauvreté de Dieu
(Pomfret, Connecticut/USA 1966)

Gebet in der Todesnähe

Der größte aller Tode, Herr,
ist der, von dem man weiß,
ist der, den man schon kennt,
der reinste aller Tode, Herr,
ist der, den man Dir weiht
und der Dir zum Opfer wird.

Ich nenne es Gnade zu wissen,
daß ich sterben muß
und daß es bald sein wird,
die Ärzte haben es mir anvertraut.
Sie sprechen von der Zeit, die mir noch bleibt,
sie sprechen von der Macht ihrer Wissenschaft,
sie sprechen von der Ohnmacht ihrer Wissenschaft,
und daß ich mich einstellen muß
auf meinen Tod.

Du segnest mich mit dieser Gnade,
denn Gnade ist die Zeit der Einkehr, die Du mir läßt,
Du segnest mich, indem Du mich in Kenntnis setzt
von Deinem Kommen.
Du hast mir eine Frist geschenkt,
in der ich mein Leben
noch einmal ordnen kann,
in der ich es noch einmal fassen kann,
um es aufzuheben vor Dein Angesicht
und es Dir darzureichen als Opfergabe.

Danke, Herr, daß ich noch fähig bin,
mich bewußt Dir hinzugeben,
jetzt, im Akt meines Selbstverzichts,
dem freiesten Akt, eines Menschen würdig.
Möge er zu einer Messe werden,
zur großen Messe meines Lebens

und zu meiner letzten,
einer Messe, bei der ich alles in allem sein werde:
Altar, Priester und Opfer.
Im Einvernehmen mit dem,
was kommen muß,
weihe ich mich Dir in diesem Gebet,
Deinem heiligen Willen weihe ich mich.
Herr, was Du auch verlangen magst,
Du hast mein Ja schon zu dieser Stunde,
es enthält meine Angst und Einsamkeit,
das ganze Gewicht dieses gefürchteten Todes.
Möge er dennoch in Liebe erlitten werden
ganz aus der Freiheit meines Wesens!

Herr, um nach deinem Willen zu bestehen,
spende mir Deine Gnade,
erfülle mich mit Gotteskraft,
gib mir vom Geist Deines göttlichen Friedens,
erfülle mein Herz mit göttlicher Freude
und laß es Deine Liebe spüren.

Dann werde ich in erleuchteter Schau
den „Bruder Tod" umarmen können
als meinen Befreier.
Er ist das Licht in der Finsternis,
das Tor zu einem neuen Morgen
und der Aufbruch ins wahre Leben
unversiegbarer Seligkeit.

In den Kelch dieser letzten Eucharistie
gieße ich mein Leiden wie einen Wein,
damit es sich mit Deinem Blut verbinde,
damit es sich mit Deinem Tod vereine.
Möge mein Opfer ganz das Deine sein!
Möge Dein Opfer ganz das meine sein!

Ist mein Leib nicht der Deine, Herr?
Ist mein Tod nicht der Deine?
Und ist meine Angst nicht auch die Deine?
Sagt man nicht, Du befändest Dich
„in Agonie bis ans Ende der Zeiten" –

in den Hospitälern der Welt
und überall dort, wo gelitten wird?

Hast Du nicht ALLES Leben auf Dich genommen?
Auch ALLES Leiden und die Verlassenheit im Tode?
Hast Du nicht ALLES Fleisch angenommen
in der Stunde der Inkarnation?
„UND DAS WORT IST FLEISCH GEWORDEN ..."
Bist Du nicht der Leidende in uns ALLEN
Und auch der Sterbende?

Herr, es tut wohl zu wissen, daß wir EIN Wesen sind
und daß Du Nacht und Not mit mir teilen wirst.
Herr, es tut wohl zu wissen, daß Du bei mir bist,
daß Du mit mir kämpfst und mit mir leiden wirst.
Ist Dein Name nicht EMMANUEL – „Gott mit uns" –
in ALLEN Phasen unseres Lebens
und in der Ewigkeit?

ALLE Schmerzen der Welt wurden verklärt
in der Wandlung, die sie durch Dich erfuhren:
Im Gnadenlicht des Ostermorgens
haben Leid und Tod ihren Sinn erhalten,
haben mein Leid und mein Tod ihren Sinn erhalten,
„TOD, WO IST DEIN SIEG? TOD, WO IST DEIN STACHEL?"

Dieses Mysterium hast Du uns enthüllt
als die Weltbotschaft für alle.
Dem Leben allein gibt sie das Letzte Wort,
„DENN DER TOD WIRD NICHT MEHR SEIN",
sie verkündet das Leben, das Du selber bist:
„ICH BIN DAS LEBEN".
Ja, Herr, Du bist mein Leben.

Original:
Pour Cornelia
(Kairo, am Ostermorgen 1989)

Die Eucharistie im Zentrum der Welt

Es war einmal ein kleiner Grashalm auf einem Hügel, der sich vergnügt im Winde wiegte und sich seines Daseins freute. Als er hungrig wurde, griff er im Erdreich nach einem Molekül und erklärte ihm:

„Gib acht, ich werde dich jetzt essen, denn ich bin hungrig ... Andererseits tust du mir herzlich leid, denn du bist sehr schön in deiner Vollkommenheit, du kleines Molekül! Wie egoistisch von mir, deinem Dasein nun ein Ende zu bereiten, damit ich leben kann ... Je länger ich dich betrachte, desto unschlüssiger werde ich ... Sollte ich dir nicht deine Freiheit lassen in der Erde, deinem Reich?"

Da sprach das Molekül:

„Nichts verstehst du! Bedenke doch, daß ich hier nicht mehr bin als nur ein Molekül. Wenn du mich aber zu dir ziehst und mich verspeist, dann werde ich lebendig, denn ich werde eine Zelle, ich werde du! Und das genau will ich schon, solang' ich denken kann: Ich will sein wie du, ein lebendiger Grashalm, tänzelnd in Wind und Sonne – und kein vergrabenes Molekül in dunkler Erde. Kannst du das verstehen? ... Bitte, nimm mich auf!"

Der kleine Grashalm hatte es verstanden, saugte das Molekül in sich hinein und ließ noch viele weitere folgen. Das Molekül war jetzt wohl als Molekül gestorben, aber als lebendige Zelle war es auferstanden in diesem Grashalm und ein Teil von ihm.

Da sprang ein kleines weißes Schäfchen daher und kletterte auf diesen Hügel. Es sah den Grashalm und bekam Appetit, gleich wollte es ihn aus der Erde rupfen. Doch plötzlich hielt es ein, tat einen Sprung zurück und sagte sich:

„Ganz unmöglich! Ich kann es nicht! Wie egoistisch von mir, dem Leben dieses glücklichen Grashalms hier in der Natur ein Ende zu bereiten ..."

Da sah der kleine Grashalm das Schäfchen bittend an und sprach: „Komm näher! ich weiß, du hast Appetit auf mich, aber zugleich hast du auch Hemmungen, mich zu verspeisen, nicht wahr? Du irrst! Bedenke doch, daß ich nur ein kleines Pflänzchen bin, unbeweglich stehe ich im Erdreich eingewurzelt ... Wenn du mich aber frißt, dann werde ich in Fleisch und Blut verwandelt, ich werde Leben, ich werde du, und ich kann durchs Grüne springen, tanzen und spielen. Sieh doch, wie ich festgehalten werde in der Erde ..."

Das kleine weiße Schäfchen hatte es verstanden, nahm den Halm und fraß ihn auf. So war der kleine Grashalm als Pflänzchen wohl gestorben, aber er lebte fort als jenes Schäfchen, das freudig über das Land sprang.

Gegen Abend lief das kleine weiße Schäfchen zurück zum Stall und traf dort den Sohn des Hauses, einen kleinen Buben, der es in seine Arme schloß und weinte. „Weshalb weinst du denn?" fragte das Schäfchen, und der Bub zog es noch fester an sein Herz und sagte:

„Morgen feiern wir ein Fest. Papa hat gesagt, daß man dich töten wird und wir dich alle essen werden."

Da sah das kleine Schäfchen den Buben mit großen Augen an und sprach:

„Und deshalb weinst du? Aber du verstehst ja gar nicht, worum es geht, mein Kind! Bitte nimm mich, bring mich zu deinem Papa, und feiert morgen euer Fest mit mir, indem ihr alle von mir eßt. Schau, jetzt bin ich nur ein kleiner Vierbeiner vom Reich der Tiere. Wenn du mich aber nimmst und ißt, dann werde ich zum F e s t , dann werde ich w i e i h r – und dann werde ich d u , ich dringe in dich ein, um endlich das zu werden, wovon ich immer träumte: EIN MENSCH."

Der Bub verstand. Er nahm das kleine weiße Schäfchen und brachte es dem Vater.

Am nächsten Tag feierten die Menschen ein Fest mit dem kleinen weißen Schäfchen. Es war jetzt wohl tot als Schäfchen, durch seinen Tod jedoch verwandelt worden in menschliche Feststimmung und Freude, in Liebe und Gemeinschaft unter den Menschen.

„Nimm mich auf in Dich!" ... Das ganze Weltmysterium drückt sich aus in diesen Szenen! Das Mysterium von Tod und Leben und der ständige Austausch in der Natur, um sich zu verwirklichen, um ans Ziel zu gelangen und sich zu vollenden. Jede Existenz einer niederen Ordnung sehnt sich danach, von einem höheren Sein als sie selbst aufgenommen zu werden; sie will sich an das Höhere verlieren können, sie will in ihm sterben, um in ihm fortzuleben – auf immer vereint.

Das ist der Aufstieg des Minerals über die Pflanze und über das Tier zum Menschen. In der Humanisierung schließlich die letzte „Rangerhöhung" der Dinge und Wesen, der Mensch unterwirft sich durch seine Arbeit die Schöpfung, um diese zu humanisieren, er fördert sie wertmäßig. Wir denken dabei an die Nahrungsaufnahme und Nahrungsumwandlung im menschlichen Körper, an Manufaktur oder industrielle Herstellung nützlicher Objekte aus den gegebenen Rohstoffen, und wir denken auf dem Gebiet des Geistes an alle Kunst und Erkenntnis. Es ist das Ziel der Dinge und Wesen, vermenschlicht zu werden, in der Bewegungslinie ihrer natürlichen Entwicklung können sie jedoch diese höhere Ebene von sich aus nicht erreichen. Irgendwann bleiben sie am Wege ihres evolutionären Aufstiegs stehen, und der Mensch muß sie dort an ihrem Standort erfassen, sie aufheben zu sich und sie humanisieren.

Macht euch die Erde untertan!

(Genesis 1)

Dieses Verwandlungsgeschehen, das der Mensch durch seine Arbeit leistet, ist priesterliches Tun. Der Mensch ist Priester der Schöpfung. Ferner ist es die Berufung der Dinge, den Menschen in seinem geistigen Wachstum zu fördern und ihm zu helfen, sich selbst heranzubilden. Die Nahrungsaufnahme von Mineral, Pflanze und Tier als Lebensstoffe ist nur ein Beispiel, denn alle biologischen, manuellen oder intellektuellen Umwandlungen führen den Menschen letztlich zur geistigen Erkenntnis. Also dient die Schöpfung dem Menschen, und die Beziehung ist eine gegenseitige.

Hält nun aber die Bewegung dort an, wo das Kind das Schäfchen in sich aufnimmt? Steht der Mensch am Gipfel und Endpunkt der Schöpfung? Gibt es nicht noch ein uns überlegenes Wesen, zu dem wir wiederum sagen könnten: „Nimm mich auf in Dich!"? Seltsamerweise hat es vor sehr langer Zeit jemanden gegeben, der genau diese Worte umgekehrt, nämlich an uns, den Menschen, gerichtet hat:

Nehmet hin und esset, das ist Mein Leib!

(Matthäus 26, 27b)

Wer mich ißt, wird durch Mich leben.

(Johannes 6, 57b)

Wer Mein Fleisch ißt und Mein Blut trinkt,
der bleibt in Mir und Ich in ihm.

(Johannes 6, 56)

Das hat die Zuhörer sehr schockiert, und sie empörten sich. Johannes berichtet:

Da murrten die Juden und stritten untereinander. Wie kann uns dieser sein Fleisch
zu essen geben?
Er aber sprach zu ihnen:
Wenn ihr das Fleisch des Menschensohnes
nicht essen und sein Blut nicht trinken werdet,
so werdet ihr das Leben nicht in euch haben;
wer Mein Fleisch ißt und Mein Blut trinkt,
hat ewiges Leben, und Ich werde Ihn auferwecken
am Jüngsten Tage.

(Johannes 6, 52-54)

Ewiges Leben – Auferstehung! ... Neue Wörter erklangen im menschlichen Ohr, und man fragte sich, was sie bedeuten. Kann denn das zeitliche Leben des Menschen in ein ewiges münden? Aus dem sicheren Tode soll neues Leben erwachsen? Wäre die jahrtausendealte Ahnung des Menschen am Ende Tatsächlichkeit? Wahrheit?

So ist es, denn ein neues Reich hatte begonnen! Nach dem Mineralreich, dem Pflanzenreich und dem Tierreich war in der Evolution das Reich des Menschen gefolgt. Und nun, an einem bestimmten Tag in der Geschichte dieses Menschen, manifestierte sich ein weiteres Reich, etwas vollkommen Neues: Das Gottesreich! In unserer Mitte wurde ein Mensch geboren, dessen äußere Erscheinung der unseren vollkommen glich, und doch war er mehr als nur ein Mensch. Es verhielt sich geradeso wie mit dem ersten Menschen auf dieser Erde, dessen Äußeres wohl kaum vom Gorilla oder Schimpansen zu unterscheiden war, aber versteckt in seinem Innern trug er den Funken des Geistes. Dieser Geistfunke war das Zeichen eines neuen, erwachenden Reiches, des Menschenreiches. Dieser Geistfunke sollte die Welt verändern und unseren Planeten vollkommen umgestalten. Doch sofort erkennbar war dieser erste Mensch und all seine verborgenen Schätze anfangs nicht gewesen. So wurde auch der Gründer des Gottesreiches als nur ein Mensch betrachtet, ein Mensch wie jeder andere ...

Dieser neue Mensch trug nicht nur den Geistfunken, sondern das Gottesreich in seinem Innern, eine ganz neue Wirklichkeit, die die Welt erschütterte. Dieser Mensch ist Jesus Christus, Herz und Achse der Geschichte, „den beide Testamente als ihr Zentrum ansehen, das Alte Testament als seine Erwartung und das Neue als sein Vorbild" (Pascal).

Öffne ein Lexikon auf beliebiger Seite und suche einen beliebigen Namen oder ein beliebiges Ereignis in der Geschichte, und Du wirst es in Beziehung gesetzt finden zu diesem Menschen: „vor Christus", „nach Christus". Dieser bescheidene und unbekannte Zimmermann aus einem unbekannten Dorf in einer unbekannten Gegend ist unser Zentrum geworden und unsere Richtung. War er sich dessen bewußt? Hören wir ihn:

Ich bin der Weg, die Wahrheit und das Leben.

(Johannes 14)

Ich bin die Tür.

(Johannes 10)

Ich bin der gute Hirte.

(Johannes 10)

Ich bin der Weinstock, ihr die Reben.

(Johannes 15)

Ich bin euer Herr und Meister.

(Johannes 13)

Ich bin das Licht der Welt.

(Johannes 8)

Ich bin der Menschensohn.

(Matthäus 18)

Ich bin das Reich Gottes.

(Matthäus 12)

Ich bin der Christus, der Sohn des lebendigen Gottes.

(Matthäus 16)

Ich bin die Auferstehung und das Leben.

(Johannes 11)

Ich bin das ALPHA und das OMEGA,
der Erste und der Letzte,
der Anfang und das Ende.

(Offenbarung 22)

Ich bin der Lebendige.

(Offenbarung 1)

Welche Beziehung aber besteht nun zwischen dem kleinen Grashalm und seiner Geschichte und diesem Welt-Meister, diesem Haupt, das den Zug der Menschheit anführt, dem ewigen Leben entgegen? ... Er hat sich dem unergründlichen Weltgesetz unterworfen, das man den „Tod" nennt, um durch sein Sterben die unendliche Zahl der menschlichen Wesen aufnehmen zu können und sie in sich zu vereinen. Wie das in die Erde fallende Weizenkorn zunächst sterben muß, um die im Boden verstreuten Moleküle anziehen und aufnehmen zu können, so mußte der Menschensohn sich auf der Erde inkarnieren, sterben und begraben werden, um alle Moleküle in sich zu vereinen, die wir Menschen sind.

Wahrlich, Ich sage euch: Wenn das Weizen-
korn nicht in die Erde fällt und stirbt,
so bleibt es für sich allein; wenn es
aber stirbt, bringt es reiche Frucht.

(Johannes 12, 24)

Und einige Zeilen später lesen wir, wie er das Sterben auf sich selbst bezieht und uns ein Versprechen gibt:

Wenn Ich von der Erde erhöht bin,
werde Ich alle an Mich ziehen.

(Johannes 12, 32)

Jesus Christus ist der am Karfreitag in die Erde gefallene Same, der sterbend die menschlichen Moleküle absorbiert wie jener Grashalm in unserer kleinen Legende. Er zieht die Menschheit in sich ein, wir werden eins mit ihm, und er läßt uns aufwachsen zu einem weitverzweigten Baum, er läßt uns zusammenwachsen zu einem Reich – zu seinem Reich.

Diese Integration durch Tod und Auferstehung Christi vollzieht sich unaufhörlich in den Mysterien von Taufe und Eucharistie. Wir werden mit ihm zu einem Leib, zu seinem Leib.

Während des eucharistischen Mahles haben wir freilich den Eindruck, Christus in uns aufzunehmen, doch das ist ein Irrtum. Nicht wir empfangen ihn, sondern er empfängt uns! Nicht er, „der liebe Jesus", verbindet sich unter dem Zeichen der kleinen Hostie mit uns, sondern wir gehen durch die unsererseits bewußt vollzogene Kommunion ein in den kosmisch großen Christus, der uns unermeßlich übersteigt, der uns alle umfaßt und in sich aufnimmt. Er sammelt uns ein in seinen Armen, und wir werden eins mit seinem Wesen. Jeder von uns wird als lebende Zelle zu einem Teil dieses kosmischen Christusleibes.

Jesus Christus ist das einzige Prinzip, das groß und weit, vollkommen und universal genug ist, die Menschheitsmoleküle zu absorbieren und in sich zu vereinen. Die gegenwärtige Menschheit sucht ihre Einheit. Immer frappierender sind die neuesten Meldungen über modernste Telekommunikationstechnik, und phantastisch klingen die Beschreibungen von Transportmitteln unserer nahen Zukunft, an denen gearbeitet wird. Ein Kommunikationsnetz webt sich und spannt sich über unseren Planeten, und seine Maschen werden dichter und dichter, um die Distanz zwischen den Menschen mehr und mehr zu verringern. In Wahrheit aber sind die Menschen nicht besser verbunden, wenn sie räumlich einander näherrücken und sich immer schneller und immer bequemer erreichen können. Wir wissen um die Einsamkeit in der Menge, wir haben die Erfahrung mit dem nahen Feind und dem fernen Freund. Obwohl der Orient nur noch wenige Flugstunden von Europa entfernt liegt, ist er doch Europa nicht näher gekommen oder gar wesensmäßig mit ihm vereint. Wirkliche Nähe ist nicht eine Frage räumlicher Entfernung, und die wahre Einheit können unsere technischen Wunderwerke nicht schaffen ...

Das einzige, das uns einander näherbringt, ist die Liebe. Und diese Liebe ist die Person Jesus Christus. Nur in ihm wird die Menschheit eines Tages ihre wahre und vollkommene Einheit finden. Die Aggregation eines Steinblocks, d. h. die bloße Anhäufung von Molekülen, ist ja doch etwas völlig anderes als eine geschaffene neue Wesenheit durch den Aufstieg in ein höheres Prinzip.

Das Evangelium bleibt daher die aktuellste Botschaft für unsere Welt. Das Christentum ist keine Religion von gestern und vorgestern, sondern eine Religion des Heute, des Morgen und des Übermorgen.

Original:
L' Eucharistie au centre du monde
(Rivière-du-Loup/Kanada 1966)

Der Geist wirkt im Verborgenen

So wie sich der organische Leib Christi unter der Einwirkung des Geistes im Leib der Maria gebildet hatte, so bildet sich auch der eucharistische Leib Christi unter der Einwirkung desselben Geistes auf dem Altar. So wie sich der mystische Leib Christi unter der Einwirkung des Geistes im Abendmahlsaal in Jerusalem gebildet hatte, so bildet sich auch der eucharistische Leib Christi unter der Einwirkung dieses Geistes unter den Menschen während der Messe.

Alles trägt das Siegel des Geistes, alles wird bestimmt und geführt durch sein aktives Leben im Innern der Dinge und Wesen, der Geist ist wirkende Anwesenheit. Seit dem ersten Augenblick des Schöpfungsbeginns treffen wir auf den Geist: *„Der Geist schwebte über den Gewässern der Urflut"* (Genesis 1), und wir lesen, daß er eine höchste Rolle spielte bei der Erschaffung des Menschen: *„Gott blies ihm Lebensodem ein"* (Genesis 2). Und wer die Geschichte des israelitischen Volkes verfolgt und dabei nach dem Geist forscht, dem wird er sich gewiß in den Worten der großen Propheten zu erkennen geben. Später, am Jordanufer, eine neue Offenbarung: Johannes der Täufer erlebt ihn im Moment der Taufe Jesu: *„Ich sah den Geist wie eine Taube aus dem Himmel niedersteigen und über ihm (Jesus) schweben"* Johannes 1, 32). Und schließlich legt der sterbende Jesus auf Golgotha den Geist in die Hände des Vaters. Am historischen Pfingsttag, lesen wir, ging der Geist unter Sturmgetöse als Flammenzungen auf die Apostel nieder und machte neue Menschen aus ihnen. Seit diesem Tag lebt und wirkt und schafft der Geist, so wie es uns versprochen wurde, in allen Kirchen Christi auf Erden.

Vom Vater sprechen, heißt von der Schöpfung sprechen. Vom Sohn sprechen, heißt von der Inkarnation sprechen. Vom Geist sprechen, heißt von der Kirche sprechen und von der Heiligwerdung der Menschheit. Wie man das Alte Testament das Evangelium des Vaters nennt und das Neue das Evangelium des Sohnes, so kann man die Geschichte der Kirche das Evangelium des Geistes nennen.

Doch trennen wir diese Begriffe nicht zu scharf, denn die Dreifaltigkeit ist, wie wir wissen, in der Einheit am Wirken; in jedem dieser drei genannten Begriffe ist sie ganz enthalten. Dennoch erkennen wir gemeinsam mit den großen Kirchenvätern eine Art Vorrang dieser oder jener der drei göttlichen Personen auf den drei großen Etappen des Heilsweges der Menschheit.

Den Geist finden wir in der Herzmitte aller kirchlichen Entwicklung, und während der Messe werden wir hineingenommen in den Ablauf eines grandiosen und bewegenden Geistgeschehens. Wir werden in ihm als Menschen gewürdigt, da uns der Vater in ihm erschaffen hat – im Geiste! Im Geist werden wir vom Sohn am Kreuz erkauft – und während der Messe erleben wir, wie der Geist uns teilnehmen läßt an den Früchten der Erlösung. Wir erkennen, daß er es ist, der uns heilig macht. Wir erleben das Kreuzesopfer Jesu, und sein Tod erkauft der Welt das Heil. In einem bestimmten Sinn ist die ganze Welt in dieser dunklen Todesstunde bereits eingelöst und errettet worden. In einem andern Sinn aber, nicht weniger wahr, ist offensichtlich noch nichts getan, Welt und Mensch warten noch darauf, sicht- und fühlbar erlöst zu werden. Dieses göttliche Heil wirkt sich in der Schöpfung – in Raum und Zeit – erst langsam aus, und es wird durch die Einwirkung des Geistes an sein Ziel gebracht und vollendet. Es ist seine Leistung, ohne den Geist käme das Christusopfer nicht zur Vollendung.

In erlösender Weise war der Geist bereits auf Golgotha anwesend: *„Vater, in Deine Hände empfehle ich meinen Geist."* Diese johanneische Ausdrucksweise muß unbedingt wörtlich genommen werden, denn hier wird klar, daß sich der all-erlösende Geist schon am Karfreitag über die Welt ergoß – das wir die Geburt der Kirche aus den Wunden Jesu nennen – und daß Pfingsten schon hier am Kreuz stattgefunden hat. Pfingsten unter dem Kreuz. Das spätere Pfingstereignis unter Flammenzeichen und Sprachwundern für die Apostel war der raum-zeitliche Ausdruck dessen, was IM GEISTE schon geschehen war. Jetzt hatte es sich geschichtlich manifestiert.

Dasselbe Phänomen erkennen wir bei Christi Himmelfahrt in Beziehung zum Auferstehungsereignis. Ist Christus nicht sofort am Tage seiner Auferstehung in den Himmel eingegangen? Aber wir Menschen denken in Schritten und Etappen, da wir als Geschöpfe in der zeitlicher Dimension leben und empfinden.

All das erlaubt uns, den Sinn der Geist-Anrufung am Altar besser zu verstehen, denn immer und überall arbeitet der Geist auf dieselbe Weise. Ich glaube daher, daß im Moment der Wandlung von Brot und Wein der Geist stillschweigend bereits am Werke ist noch vor meinem ersten Priesterwort, denn ohne den Geist käme es ohnehin zu keiner Wandlung. Er lebt und wirkt im Innersten dieses Prozesses, er ist der Hauptagent. Aber so wie wir Menschen nicht alles auf einmal sagen können, so wird auch die Rolle des Geistes hier in einem besonderen Ritus etappenweise vollzogen, ein Ritus, der dieses Opferereignis betrifft. Natürlich ändern die rituellen Priesterworte substantiell nichts am Opfer selbst, das sich hier geheimnisvoll vollendet, sondern sie offenbaren jetzt dieses Geschehen.

Dennoch glauben wir nicht, daß diese Wort-Manifestation etwas Nebensächliches ist, auf das man vielleicht verzichten könnte. Weit entfernt! Eine solche Sicht würde die wahre und tiefe Bedeutung der Liturgie verkennen. Die Liturgie der Messe entfaltet in der Zeit einen Augenblick, der ontologisch (im Sein) ein einziger Augenblick ist, substantiell unteilbar. Wenn man dieses Zeit-Entfalten versteht und ihm zustimmt, dann muß man ihm auch alle seine Dimensionen zugestehen und zwar in einer harmonischen Offenbarung aller seiner wesentlichen Bestandteile. Geben wir acht, daß wir die Liturgie nicht beschneiden! Die Herabrufung des Geistes auf die Gaben des Altars ist nur ein Teil der Liturgie. Lösen wir nichts aus ihr heraus, wir könnten sonst schwere Fehler zu bereuen haben.

Jetzt können wir auch besser erkennen, weshalb die orientalische Kirche besonderen Akzent auf die Anrufung des Geistes legt und weshalb die lateinische Kirche mehr die Wandlung selbst betont. Welche Kirche hat recht? Natürlich beide Kirchen, jede auf ihre Weise. Substantiell und rechtlich gesehen hat die lateinische Kirche recht, wenn sie sagt, daß die Weiheworte des Priesters die Wandlung bewirken. Liturgisch und dogmatisch gesehen hat die orientalische Kirche recht, denn sie gibt dem Geist seinen wahren Platz im eucharistischen Opfer.

Wer aber ist dieser Geist nun tatsächlich?

Wir nennen ihn „Person". Sprechen wir von der Person des Vaters, dann fällt es uns verhältnismäßig leicht, uns eine Vorstellung zu machen, ohne daß wir ein Attribut wie einen weißen Bart heranziehen müssen ... Ohne Schwierigkeit erkennen wir ihn als Quelle und Ursprung des Sohnes und der Dreifaltigkeit. Der biblische Schöpfungsmythos und die Geschichte des israelitischen Volkes erlauben uns, sein Tun und Wirken zu verfolgen und seine „Psychologie" zu erfassen, wenn man so sagen darf. Und die Person des Sohnes ist uns in den vier glänzenden Porträts der Evangelisten gezeichnet worden. Anschaulicher und ergreifender können wir uns das Bild des Gottessohnes und Menschensohnes weder denken noch wünschen. Aber der Geist? ... Wer vermag über die Person des Geistes ähnlich anschauliche Aussagen zu machen? Unser Verlangen nach einer guten Vorstellung bleibt unbefriedigt. Weshalb ist der Geist derart geheimnisvoll?

Zunächst könnte man antworten, daß das Wesentliche und Typische dieses Mittlers sein Verschwinden ist. Angesichts der Elemente, die er miteinander verbindet, tritt er zurück ins Unerkennbare. Innerhalb der Dreifaltigkeit ist er das Liebesband zwischen Vater und Sohn, die Liebesenergie, die Liebesfunktion, und das ist tatsächlich die Rolle des Geistes auch in der Kirche: Liebende Mittlerrolle – selbst aber unbestimmbar, unfaßbar – und deshalb in dieser Stärke wirksam!

Der Geist ist die im Geheimen wirkende, aber eigentliche Energie, die entgegengesetzten Polen erlaubt, zu einer unauflöslichen Einheit zu verschmelzen. Der Geist ist jenes geheime Leben, das die unzählbaren Zellen eines Baumes oder eines menschlichen Körpers zum harmonischen Einen formt und zusammenhält. Der Geist ist das Fundamentalprinizp allen Lebens, allen Seins, und man sieht nichts von ihm! Er ist Quelle und Seele allen Seins, allen Werdens, und er bleibt doch unerreichbar für uns.

Wundern wir uns daher nicht, daß uns der Geist mysteriös erscheint in seinem Wirken und Schaffen als Quelle und Seele der Kirche. Denn in Wahrheit ist das Mysterium des Geistes ein Mysterium innigster Intimität. Nicht der Geist ist Illusion, sondern seine vermutete Abwesenheit ist Illusion unsererseits. Wenn er sich unseren menschlichen Vorstellungen und intelligenten Recherchen dann und wann entzieht, dann bedeutet das nicht, daß er uns fern sei, sondern daß er dann vielleicht gerade in verstärktem Maße tief in unserm Innern an der Arbeit ist. Der Geist spricht aus den Tiefenzonen unseres Wesens zu uns, wird aber nur von dem verstanden, der sich reinigt und läutert und der in seinem Herzen eine entsprechende Stille zu bereiten weiß, denn der Geist wirkt im Verborgenen.

Eine andere Begründung für die Unfaßlichkeit und unbegreiflichkeit des Wesens der dritten Person der Dreifaltigkeit ist der ungeschlossene Bereich ihres Wirkens. Überall ist der Geist intensiv an der Arbeit, sowohl in der Kirche als außerhalb von ihr, um den globalen menschlichen Teig wie durch Hefe anzuheben bis zu seiner vollen Reife.

Paulus lehrt uns, daß *„die gesamte Schöpfung in der Erwartung der Offenbarung der Gottessöhne seufzt"*. Wer sind die Gottessöhne, die erwartet werden? Wir alle! Wir alle sind gemeint, und der Geist ist jene geheimnisvolle Macht, die das Wachstum in diese Vollendung hinein bewirkt. Je deutlicher das Gottesreich auf Erden in Erscheinung tritt, umso klarer wird sich auch der Geist offenbaren und von immer mehr Menschen erkannt werden. Und wenn die Welt eines Tages in der „Fülle der Zeit" stehen wird, wenn die endgültige Ankunft des Herrn von allen erlebt wird, dann wird der Geist in seiner ganzen Kraft und in seinem vollen Glanz sichtbar werden – für alle!

Die Geschichte der Kirche ist für dieses Geistgeschehen vorläufig symbolisch, denn sie ist die langsame „Inkarnation" des Geistes. Solange diese „Inkarnation" noch nicht vollkommen ist, wird der Geist geheimnisvoll verborgen bleiben. Und was uns getaufte Christen betrifft, so ist es unsere heilige Pflicht und Verantwortung, diese „Inkarnation" des Geistes in der Welt nach allen Kräften zu fördern – in unserer Umgebung wie in unserem eigenen Herzen. Der Geist bildet das Zentrum der Kirche, und so muß er auch unser Zentrum werden, voll bewußt und alle Tage innig von uns gelebt. Der Geist muß fühlbar eine Person für uns sein, an die wir uns in jeder Lebenssituation wenden, bei allen Fragen und wichtigen Entscheidungen.

Dann mag der Geist das Wunder einer wahren und endgültigen Bekehrung vollbringen. Die Verwandlung und Bekehrung einer einzigen Seele ist ein viel weltbewegenderes Ereignis als die Landung des Menschen auf dem Mond und ein größeres und tieferes als die Heilung eine kranken Körpers! ...

Es ist nicht genug, ein „anständiger Mensch" zu sein, wie viele von uns glauben möchten. Das ist das Mindeste, das einem Getauften abverlangt wird. Nein, ein guter Christ zu sein, ist nicht genug. Durch gute Werke seine Seele retten zu wollen – wie kann das genug sein? Die Apostel waren vor dem „wunder"-baren Pfingsttag schon gute Christen gewesen. Sie hatten alles verlassen und waren ihrem Meister gefolgt. Drei Jahre lebten sie mit ihm, teilten sein einfaches und schwieriges Leben mit ihm und hörten von Person zu Person jedes Wort, das er sagte. Aber all das war nicht genug gewesen. Jetzt wurde es notwendig, diese Männer auf eine höhere Stufe des Christseins zu heben, auf die Stufe der Heiligkeit und des Zeugnisgebens. Es ging um sehr viel mehr! Es ging nicht nur um das Haben der christlichen Lehre, sondern um das Sein und um das Geben aus dem Sein.

Dem Christen darf es nicht allein darum gehen, sich selbst zu retten, sondern mit ihm die andern. Dieser Auftrag an die Apostel erforderte eine tiefe und totale Umwandlung ihres Wesens. Auch wir müssen „aufgehoben werden" auf ein höheres chistliches Niveau, wir alle! Auch wir dürfen nicht nur uns selber im Auge haben und ein christliches Dasein zur eigenen Rettung führen, sondern dieses christliche Dasein muß sich ausrichten auf die andern.

Paulus lehrt uns, daß niemand für sich allein lebt und daß niemand für sich allein stirbt. Das bedeutet, daß wir für die andern verantwortlich sind. Wir sind ein grüner Zweig am Baum des Heils, und viele Blätter leben von uns. Wenn wir das Leben, das wir vom Stamm erhalten, nicht an alle erreichbaren Blätter weiterleiten, dann werden sie aufgrund unserer Unterlassungssünde absterben.

Niemand ist eine Insel. Niemand lebt so isoliert, daß seine persönliche Verhaltensweise nur ihn selber betrifft. Niemand ist so unabhängig, daß sich sein Tun und Denken allein auf ihn bezieht. Nein, die ganze Welt wird betroffen von meinen geheimsten und tiefsten Gedanken und Entschlüssen. Die ganze Welt wird betroffen von meinen ganz privaten und persönlichen Lebensäußerungen. Niemand ist eine Insel.

Bitte, lieber Freund, sage Dir niemals:

> Ich habe keine Theologie studiert.
> Ich bin nur ein einfacher Mensch.
>
> Ich bin eine überbeschäftigte Hausfrau,
> ich habe keine Zeit und keine Möglichkeit.

Ich bin Medizinstudent.
Theologie ist nicht mein Fachgebiet.

Ich bin nichts als ein Laie.
Welchen Beitrag soll ich leisten können?

Darauf sage ich Dir:

> Es ist vollkommen uninteressant, was Du bist und was Du gelernt hast, wenn es darum geht, Apostel Christi zu werden. Jeder kann es, wenn er das richtige Herz dafür hat, das um den Geist zu bitten versteht. Es spielt überhaupt keine Rolle, was Du rechtmäßig gelernt hast. Was zählt, ist allein der Heiligkeitsgrad, den Du in Deinem Leben erreichst. Ferner ist es unwesentlich, wieviel Zeit Dir Dein Alltag für ein Apostolat läßt, denn fruchtbringend ist ohnehin nur die Intensität Deines Einsatzes.

Die Apostel hatten kein Doktorat der Theologie in der Tasche, als sie zu predigen begannen. Auch hatten sie kein jahrelanges Laienstudium in Bibliotheken betrieben, als sie apostolisch zu wirken begannen. Die meisten unter ihnen wußten wohl nicht einmal ihren Namen zu schreiben. Gerade deshalb hat der Herr sie auserwählt, denn hierdurch wurde für die Welt offenbar, daß es nicht ihr Werk sei, sondern das Werk des Heiligen Geistes.

Der Geist ist seitdem die Seele der Kirche und die Seele jeder einzelnen Zelle, die sich für die wachsende Kirche engagiert. Sie bilden zusammen einen Leib – das lebende Zeugnis für die Heiligkeit des Vaters und für die Liebe des Sohnes.

> Wenn der Geist in uns ist, dann ist auch
> das Wort, von dem wir ihn empfangen,
> in uns, und im Wort ist auch der Vater.
> Wo nämlich das Licht ist, da ist auch sein Glanz,
> und wo der Glanz ist, da ist auch sein Wirken
> und seine strahlende Gnade. (Anastasius)

Zeilen, die vom Patriarchen von Alexandria im 4. Jahrhundert geschrieben wurden.

Bitten wir für die Ausgießung des Heiligen Geistes in unsere Herzen, beten wir leise den Pfingst-Hymnus: „Komm, Heiliger Geist, und entzünde in uns das Feuer Deiner göttlichen Liebe ...", sodaß der Geist aus uns nicht nur gute Christen, sondern heilige Apostel mache und aus unserem Leben einen wahren Dienst am anderen – und damit am Gottesreich. Komm, heiliger Geist, verwandle uns in Deine leidenschaftlichen Mitarbeiter, überzeugend für die, denen wir ein Beispiel geben.

Original:
Le Mystère de l' Esprit/Epiclèse (Beirut/Libanon 1963);
Come, Holy Spirit ... (Chicago/USA 1966)

Ökumene und Weltkirche der Zukunft

Die katholische Kirche glaubte bis zum Zweiten Vatikanischen Konzil, über das Monopol der Wahrheit zu verfügen und den Heiligen Geist allein zu besitzen. Etwa fünzehn Jahrhunderte hindurch war das ohne größere Probleme gutgegangen, denn gut war die Ehe, die Kirche und Staat miteinander führten; Glaube und Kultur gingen im Gleichschritt und hielten sich gegenseitig, die Kirche war Schirmherrin und Förderin der Wissenschaften und Künste.

Mit der Renaissance, der protestantischen Reform und dem allgemeinen Aufbruch in die moderne Zeit brach diese Einheit zwischen Kirche und Gesellschaft, zwischen Kultur und Glaube, zwischen Religion und Wissenschaften auseinander. Mensch und Welt hatten sich plötzlich als mündig erkannt, woraufhin mehr oder weniger rasch fortschreitend die Weisungen von Mutter Kirche ignoriert wurden.

Aufgrund dieses Verlustes nahm die katholische Kirche eine starre Haltung ein, sie wurde mißtrauisch und übte Widerspruch und Verurteilung gegenüber jeder neuen Idee; die Fälle der Exkommunikation und des Bannfluchs häuften und multiplizierten sich, wobei sich die Kirche immer mehr in sich verschloß. Der Prozeß Galileis im 16. Jahrhundert war der Beginn einer langen Serie anderer Verurteilungen:

Die Verurteilung der Reformatoren, die Verurteilung der Verfechter des Darwinismus, die Verurteilung der Kämpfer für eine katholische Sozialbewegung, die Verurteilung der Anhänger und Verkünder des Modernismus in seiner Vielfalt neuer Bewegungen, die Verurteilung der progressiven Exegeten, die für eine neue Lesart der Bibel eintraten, d.h. für eine historisch-kritische Exegese unter Berücksichtigung des kulturellen und sozialen Kontextes, in dem diese Texte entstanden waren ...

Und zur selben Zeit verkündete die katholische Kirche neue Dogmen: die absolute Autorität und Unfehlbarkeit des Papstes (1870 durch Pius IX.) oder neue mariologische Dogmen wie Marias Erbsündefreiheit, auch Unbefleckte Empfängnis genannt (1854 durch Pius IX.) sowie Marias Aufnahme „ganz und ungeteilt", in die Herrlichkeit Gottes (1950 durch Pius XII.), wodurch sich der Graben zwischen der römischen Kirche und den anderen christlichen Kirchen noch mehr vertiefte. So war die orthodoxe Kirche durch das Entstehen einer katholischen Ostkirche als „Parallelerscheinung" schon tief verletzt worden, insbesondere durch den katholischen Bekehrungseifer und die Versuche einer allgemeinen Latinisierung der gesamten Ostkirche, begleitet vom weltweiten missionarischen Dienst im Namen Roms.

Die ersten zaghaften Schritte einer Öffnung der katholischen Kirche gegenüber der Neuzeit begannen schon mit der Enzyklika „Rerum Novarum" Papst Leos XIII. im Jahre 1892 über die wirtschaftlichen und sozialen Weltprobleme und mit der Enzyklika „Divino Afflante Spiritu" Papst Pius XII. im Jahre 1943, in der dieser Papst für die katholische Bibelforschung die kritische Auslegung freigab, entgegen den bisherigen einschränkenden Weisungen der Päpstlichen Bibelkommission.

Doch erst mit dem Zweiten Vatikanischen Konzil (1962-1965) nahm die katholische Kirche entschlossen eine wirklich neue Haltung ein, mitfühlend mit den andern, teilnehmend an der modernen Welt! Das war eine Neuheit in der Geschichte der Kirche, und sie setzte langsam eine Wende um 180 Grad in Gang. Was aber ist das tatsächlich Neue dieses Zweiten Vatikanischen Konzils?

Neu ist vor allem, daß dieses Konzil als erstes in der Geschichte FÜR etwas stattgefunden hatte und nicht GEGEN JEMANDEN. Diesmal befragte die Kirche SICH SELBST, und gleich in voller Tiefe, über ihre Identität, ihr Wesen und ihr Vorhaben, und sie versuchte, einen neuen Stil und eine neue Struktur sichtbar werden zu lassen. All das läßt sich im Schlüsselwort „Aggiornamento" (Modernisierung) zusammenfassen, lanciert von Papst Johannes XXIII. im Augenblick der Einberufung des Konzils.

Seitdem soll die Kirche nicht mehr verurteilen, sondern im Gegenteil, sie soll sich den vielen anderen Wahrheiten gegenüber öffnen, die außerhalb der Kirche in Erscheinung treten und auf die sie jahrhundertelang nicht zu sprechen gewesen war oder die sie gleich verurteilt hatte. Und das tat sie. Auch innerkirchlich wurde beraten über:

Das Prinzip der Kollegialität zwischen dem Papst und dem Bischofskollegium, sowie ortskirchlich zwischen dem Bischof und seiner Priesterschaft, die um ihn ein kollegiales Presbyterium bilden soll. Das Prinzip einer Meßliturgie in der jeweiligen Volkssprache, die von allen verstanden wird. Das Prinzip eines theologischen Pluralismus und die Möglichkeit, seinen christlichen Glauben in großer Vielfalt des Ausdrucks existentiell zu leben. Das Prinzip der religiösen Freiheit der Person und der Vorrang des persönlichen Gewissens des Einzelnen. Das Prinzip des Heils aller Menschen guten Willens. Das Prinzip des Dialogs mit den anderen Kirchen und mit den Nichtchristen, der nicht die Konversion oder die Zurückeroberung der anderen zum Ziel hat, sondern vielmehr die Vertiefung und Bereicherung des eigenen Mysteriums durch die Glaubensmysterien der andern ...

Der Gottesgeist überflutet ja doch in unendlichem Maß die Grenzen der sichtbaren Kirche, und der mystische Leib darf nicht mit der katholischen, apostolischen und römischen Kirche allein identifiziert werden, wie bereits aus der Enzyklika „Mystici Corporis" zu entnehmen war (1943 durch Pius XII.) – die Gesamtkirche ist der mystische Leib Christi!

Ausgehend von diesem historischen Hintergrund, der freilich sehr reich gefächert und weit entfaltet ist, möchte ich einige Ideen äußern über die Art und Weise, in der ich die Ökumene und die kirchliche Lehrtätigkeit von morgen sehe.

Die katholische Kirche ist noch nicht das, was sie vorgibt oder glaubt zu sein, sie ist noch nicht wirklich „universell". Noch immer vermittelt sie recht stark den Eindruck, eine Konfession unter anderen zu sein, eine christliche Gemeinschaft unter anderen, fixiert auf ihre eigene Vergangenheit, ihre Kultur, ihre lange Geschichte, wobei sie streng auf ihre Privilegien bedacht ist und diese eifersüchtig hütet. Mißtrauisch noch immer, befindet sie sich in einer ständigen Verteidigungsstellung gegen alles, was außerhalb ihrer Mauern keimt und grünt. Doch wird die katholische Kirche erst dann wahrhaft „katholisch" werden, wenn sie sich vorurteilslos auch dem Reichtum anderer Kofessionen, Religionen, Kulturen und Zivilisationen zu öffnen versteht. Diese Öffnung der Kirche gegenüber den unermeßlichen Schätzen des Geistes kann auf zwei Arten verstanden werden:

1. Entweder bildet die Kirche eines Tages eine höchste Weltorganisation, die alle anderen Konfessionen, Religionen und Kulturen wohlwollend integriert, d. h. gut in sich aufnimmt und verarbeitet, um eine überzentralisierte Mammutkirche für alle zu werden, an der Spitze ein Oberhaupt, der Papst von Rom, der dann als wahrer Hirte dieser Universalkirche verstanden und allseitig anerkannt wird.

2. Oder die römische Kirche verwirklicht ihre wahre Katholizität, indem sie ihre Beziehungen von Brüderlichkeit und Gemeinschaft mit den anderen Kirchen mehr und mehr entwickelt, doch ihnen ihre Autonomie, ihre Traditionen, ihre Theologie, ihre eigene Denkweise und Gebetswelt läßt. Die Kirche von Rom hätte somit als spezifische Rolle das „Präsidium der Nächstenliebe aller christlichen Kirchen" inne zu haben, jene heilige Rolle, die ihr seit dem Ursprung auferlegt ist. Der päpstliche Primat würde dann als „Dienst an der Allgemeinheit" verstanden im Gegensatz zum geschichtlichen Begriff der „Obergewalt" früherer Zeiten. Seine Autorität wäre somit eine „Rechtspflege" hinsichtlich der Einheit und der Gemeinschaft aller Menschen.

Bei diesen neuen Beziehungen zwischen den christlichen Kirchen wird es bedeutsam werden, die Gemeinschaft nicht auf den rein intellektuellen, theologisch fest abgesteckten Aspekt beschränkt zu halten, sondern sie auf alles auszuweiten, was menschlich genannt wird, d. h. alles miteinzuschließen, was das Gemüt und die Seele des Menschen bewegt und betrifft. Wenn man weiß, bis zu welchem Grad die zwischenmenschlichen Beziehungen und persönlichen Verhaltensweisen ihre Rolle bei den diversen Schismen (Glaubensspaltungen) gespielt haben, dann ist es wohl kaum notwendig, die Bedeutung der menschlichen Haltung und persönlichen spirituellen Führung hervorzuheben, welche die Gemeinschaft ausmachen und in sich vereinen: Liebe, Demut, Güte, Verständnis und Respekt für die Empfindungen (und Empfindlichkeiten!) der anderen, Respekt für die innere Harmonie und die Traditionen aller Kulturen dieser Erde.

Der wahre Grund der Schismen, welcher Art auch immer, war sehr oft die selbstgefällige und herablassende Haltung Roms gewesen, und die theologischen und dogmatischen Begründungen erfolgten meist erst nachträglich, um die aufgerichtete Scheidewand zu rechtfertigen. Wenn man demnach von Gemeinschaft spricht, dann sollte man sogleich diesen neuen Aspekt im Auge haben, ganz besonders beim Dialog mit den orientalischen Kirchen, bei denen das Gemüt und die zwischenmenschliche Begegnung eine eminente Rolle spielt, eine Rolle ganz besonderer Art.

Gehen wir zurück auf die beiden Konzepte der Kirche, die ich hier bereits schematisiert dargestellt habe, die Mammutkirche als höchste christliche Institution oder die allumfassende Glaubensgemeinschaft. Welche von ihnen wird die Weltkirche der Zukunft sein?

Ich bin der Meinung, daß es abzusehen ist, daß sich die aktuelle Theologie mehr und mehr in der zweiten Richtung orientieren wird. Die Einheit der Kirche verwirklicht sich nicht durch die Vereinnahmung aller in der einen Kirche, sondern in der Gemeinschaft miteinander. Die Kirche wird erst dann wirklich „katholisch" sein, was „allumfassend" bedeutet, wenn sie „eine Kirche der Kirchen" geworden ist, um hier den Titel eines kürzlich erschienenen Buches von Pater Tillard zu verwenden. Ihre Einheit wird dann nicht mehr vom starren, gleichförmigen Typus sein, sondern sehr bunt und vielseitig in Farbe und Ausdruck, eine im schönen Sinn des Wortes „reich" gewordene Kirche.

In diesem Kontext sollte man wieder einmal das herrliche 12. Kapitel des ersten Korintherbriefes lesen, in dem Paulus die unendliche Verschiedenartigkeit der Glieder und Funktionen des EINEN Leibes und in der Einheit des EINEN Geistes beschreibt:

> *Es gibt verschiedene Zuteilungen von Geistesgaben,*
> *doch nur EINEN Geist; es gibt verschiedene Dienste,*
> *doch nur EINEN Herrn; es gibt verschieden Wirkungen,*
> *jedoch nur EINEN Gott, der alles in allen wirkt ...*

Wie der Leib zwar nur einer ist
und dennoch viele Glieder hat, und alle Glieder dieses
Leibes, soviel es deren sind, nur einen Leib ausmachen,
so ist es auch mit Christus. In einem Geiste sind wir alle
zu einem Leibe getauft, ob wir nun Juden oder Heiden sind,
Sklaven oder Freie, wir alle sind mit einem Geiste getränkt.
Besteht doch auch der Leib nicht aus einem Gliede,
sondern aus vielen.

Und spräche auch der Fuß: „Weil ich nicht Hand bin,
so gehöre ich nicht zum Leibe", würde er deshalb nicht
zum Leibe gehören? Und spräche auch das Ohr:
„Weil ich nicht Auge bin, gehöre ich nicht zum Leibe",
würde es deshalb nicht zum Leibe gehören?
Und wenn der ganze Leib nur Auge wäre,
wo bliebe das Gehör?
Und wäre der ganze Leib nur Ohr,
wo bliebe der Geruch? ...

Nun aber hat Gott einem jeden Glied am Leibe seinen
Platz gegeben, so wie Er es wollte. Wäre aber alles nur ein
einziges Glied, wo bliebe dann der Leib?
So gibt es also viele Glieder, doch nur einen Leib.
Das Auge darf nicht zur Hand sagen:
„Ich brauche dich nicht!"
Und der Kopf darf nicht zu den Füßen sagen:
„Ich brauche euch nicht!" ...
Ihr seid nun Christi Leib und Glieder, wenngleich
als Teile angesehen."

(I Korinther 12, 4-6, 12-21, 27)

Das Prinzip des Pluralismus müßte eine Vielzahl verschiedener Ausdrucksweisen enthalten, eine jede gültig und von derselben Glaubenswahrheit getragen. Ausgehend vom gemeinsamen Glaubensbekenntnis müßte ein mannigfaltiges spirituelles Leben, mannigfaltige christliche Theologien und Gottesdienst-Liturgien, ihren geographischen Orten entsprechend, blühen können, ganz den jeweiligen Kulturen und Zeiten entsprechend.

In dieser Perspektive hat die „Groupe interconfessionel des Dombes" (gegründet 1937 in Lyon) drei Prinzipien einer ökumenischen Methodenlehre ausgearbeitet:

1. Die christologische Konzentration, bestehend im Studieren unserer Divergenzen im Lichte der Person Jesu Christi und im Durchführen einer Untersuchung des Glaubens auf seine Echtheit und Rechtmäßigkeit, gemessen am Evangelium.

2. Die dogmatische Konzentration, bestehend in der Aufforderung, wohl zu unterscheiden zwischen der Glaubenssubstanz und seinen diversen äußeren Ausdrucksformen, die ja seine unverzichtbare Darstellung bedeuten, die Sichtbarwerdung des Geglaubten. Andererseits bestehend in der wissenschaftlichen Systematisierung, die dem „theologoumena" Raum gibt, d. h. der persönlichen Einstellung eines Theologen und der systematischen Darstellung seines Denkens.

3. Die Suche nach der Lösung eines aufgetretenen Konfliktes sollte uns den Anstoß geben, „nach vorne zu wachsen" und über den gegenwärtigen Zustand oder die gegenwärtig gültige Lehrmeinung hinweg einer gemeinsamen Wahrheitsfindung entgegen, einer Wahrheit, die nicht hinter uns liegt, sondern vor uns: ein mehr forderndes, reineres und ausgewogeneres Christentum.

Der Begriff des Pluralismus, von dem ich sprach, ist außerhalb aller Kirchen zu erweitern und zu entwickeln, um den gültigen und authentischen Wahrheitskern in allen Religionen, Philosophien, Ideologien und Kulturen gegenseitig anzuerkennen und anzunehmen, zumindest aber gelten zu lassen. So öffnete sich auch die Kirche der ersten Jahrhunderte und des Mittelalters gegenüber der griechischen Philosophie. Und das hat das Zweite Vatikanische Konzil wieder versucht, indem es einen ehrlichen Dialog mit allen Menschen guten Willens eröffnet hat.

Hinter dieser Haltung steht die Überzeugung, daß der Geist die Grenzen der sichtbaren Kirche weit überflutet und den unendlichen Reichtum seiner Gaben ausgießt auf die ganze Menschheit. Die zahllosen Beispiele im Alten wie im Neuen Testament bezeugen die souveräne Freiheit des göttlichen Geistes, der sich außerhalb des „Gottesvolkes" – des Alten oder des Neuen Bundes oder der offiziellen römischen Kirche – manifestiert:

Der Geist weht, wo er will,
und du weißt nicht,
von wo er kommt und wohin er geht.

(Johannes 3, 8)

Wenn die Berufung der Kirche jene ist, alles in Christus zusammenzufassen und zu einen, so kann diese Vereinigung nur durch eine wirklich ernstgemeinte und sehr aufmerksame Öffnung geschehen, demütig und geduldig gegenüber allen anderen Geistzeugnissen in dieser Welt.

KIRCHE JENSEITS DER KIRCHE! ... Die Kirche übersteigt sich ja doch selbst in ihrem Ausmaß unendlich, und Christus ist so viel weltumspannender und größer, als wir ahnen. Solange sein mystischer Leib noch nicht die wahren universellen und kosmischen Dimensionen erhalten hat, solange wird sein Erlöservorhaben noch nicht die vollkommene Verwirklichung finden können.

Original:
Oecuménisme et Ecclesiologie
(Kairo/Ägypten 1987)

Seine Religion wählen

Welche Beziehung besteht heute zwischen Kirche und Welt? Kam es nicht längst zum endgültigen Bruch zwischen beiden, und brachte dieser Bruch für die religiöse Haltung des Menschen nicht eine ganze Skala von Konsequenzen?

Der moderne Mensch kann seine Religion nicht mehr als ein Erbgut verstehen, das er mit geschlossenen Augen passiv übernimmt, so wie er es in der theokratischen Gesellschaft des christlichen und mohammedanischen Mittelalters tat, ein Menschentypus übrigens, der noch immer in weiten Bereichen am Leben ist.

Nein, die Religion von morgen wird eine selbstgewählte Religion sein, bewußt vom Menschen angenommen oder wieder aufgenommen. Sie wird nicht mehr aufgedrängt und eingezwängt werden, und vor allem wird sie nicht mehr „erlitten", sondern herzlich frei gewünscht werden! Diese zukünftige Wahl erfordert jedoch schon heute eine entsprechende Reflexion, gezieltes Studium und viel Forschung als unumgängliche Forderungen. Der Glaube soll ein freier und bewußter Akt des mündig gewordenen Menschen werden. Die persönliche Religion wird die traditionelle ablösen.

Eine weitere Konsequenz der Scheidung von Kirche und Staat ist allen offenkundig. Die religiös geprägten kulturellen Institutionen sind am Verschwinden und werden von rein staatlichen ersetzt. Das „Weltliche" drückt täglich deutlicher seinen Stempel ins gesellschaftliche Leben, so stark, daß der Mensch in diesem Klima immer weniger an sein religiöses Leben erinnert und bei Bedarf von ihm unterstützt werden kann. Filme, Illustrierte, Schulen, Vereine und Institutionen jeglicher Art befinden sich längst außer Reichweite und Einflußnahme durch die religiösen Instanzen, und damit ist es dem Individuum völlig allein überlassen, sich abzuschirmen oder entsprechend zu reagieren, sich religiös zu informieren, das Angebot zu durchdenken und dann zu wählen.

Manche unter uns nennen das eine schlechte Entwicklung, diese neuen Umstände bezeichnen sie als negativ. Sind sie aber nicht im Grunde ein Antrieb zur tieferen Reifung und ein Appell zur größeren Selbstverantwortlichkeit und demnach eine sehr fruchtbringende Herausforderung an den heutigen Menschen? Die äußeren Strukturen müssen jetzt durch innere ersetzt werden, und die gesellschaftliche und konventionelle Moral durch eine selbst durchdachte, besonnene, persönliche Moral.

Doch ist diese Passage von der traditionellen Religion zu einer persönlichen bisher nur ein Aspekt der Veränderung, den wir in diesem Bereich beobachten. Ein anderer Aspekt, nicht weniger bedeutsam, ist die Verpflichtung des heutigen Christen, sein Christentum in eine weiteres Feld zu verlagern als bisher, nämlich in ein gemeinsames Feld mit allen anderen Religionen der Erde.

Keinesfalls darf diese Begegnung im „aggressiven Geist" glühenden Bekehrungseifers geschehen, streitend und erobernd, sondern in einer milden, gütigen und offenen Haltung, ohne die wir aufhören, Christen zu sein. Diese Haltung wird uns nicht nur im Namen der Toleranz oder der Nächstenliebe abverlangt, sondern im Namen der Redlichkeit und Wahrheit.

Wir haben von den anderen Religionen etwas zu erwarten – und zweifellos nicht wenig, denn sie sind in einem sehr wahren und tiefen Sinn Teil unserer eigenen Religion. Unser Christentum wird nur wirklich christlich werden, wenn es alle Werte der anderen Religionen der Erde in sich versammelt und miteinander verbindet.

Daher ist das Christentum nicht, wie man viel zu lange geglaubt hat, den anderen Religionen gegenüber exklusiv, d. h. sie ausschließend, sondern inklusiv, sie miteinschließend. Um wahrhaft „katholisch" zu sein, was übersetzt „universell" bedeutet, muß das Christentum allumfassend werden, das heißt alles andere mitumarmend. In diesem Sinne kann man in voller Wahrheit sagen, daß das Christentum nicht eine Religion unter anderen ist, sondern ihre Synthese.

Aus all dem ergibt sich eine neue Haltung des modernen Christen gegenüber den anderen Religionen: Um wirklich „christlich" zu sein und im Namen des Christentums wirksam zu werden, wird der

Christ zunächst innerlich Moslem werden müssen, um in ganzer Tiefe die Erfahrung des Islam zu machen, um diesen starken Herzschlag zu spüren und ihn wohl zu verstehen. Er wird innerlich Hindu und Buddhist werden und an den Weisheitsquellen asiatischer Mystik trinken müssen, um zu erleben, daß sich ihm dort ein Teil seiner eigenen Seele offenbart. Er wird innerlich afrikanischer Animist werden und bis ins Herz der Naturgeheimnisse vordringen müssen, um die heilige Gemeinschaft mit der Welt wiederzufinden, die den Naturvölkern seit jeher vertraut ist. Er wird mit einem weiten und offenen Geist zu allen Menschen gehen müssen, nicht als Lehrer einer Lehre, sondern als neugieriger Schüler des Lebens, d. h. in einer Haltung lernbegieriger Aufgeschlossenheit und Aufnahmebereitschaft. Die Wahrheit des Christentums ist kein Schatz, den man besitzt und sorgsam hütet, sondern ein langer Weg, den man geht , und eine Erfahrung, die man macht. Daß diese Erfahrung ein gewisses Risiko enthält, weil bereits Erworbenes verlorengehen könnte, ist wahr, und hier wird das Risiko sogar mehr als woanders zum Bestandteil des ganzen Unternehmens, aber

wer sein Leben liebt, wird es verlieren,
doch wer sein Leben in dieser Welt haßt,
der wird es für das ewige Leben bewahren.

(Johannes 12, 25)

So wie wir eben noch einer Art Pflicht- und Straf-Ethik preisgegeben waren, so befinden wir uns jetzt auf dem Wege zu einer Religion des Risikos – einer ganz neu erscheinenden Religion, die jedoch so alt ist wie das Evangelium selbst. Nachdem wir dann alle menschenmöglichen Wege zu Gott, die ja die verschiedenen Religionen darstellen, durchlaufen sind, sie im ernsten Verlangen nach Wahrheitserkenntnis von innen erlebt haben, wird der Christ vielleicht erkennen, daß der Abstand zwischen Himmel und Erde und zwischen dem Schöpfer und seinem Geschöpf zu unendlich ist, um jemals vom Menschen her überschritten werden zu können. Dann leuchtet ihm vielleicht der wahre Sinn des Christentums auf: Seine Religion ist keine Religion unter anderen, und sei es die beste, die ihm begegnet ist; sie ist kein zusätzlicher Weg zu Gott, und sei es der privilegierteste, sondern sie ist ein plötzliches, himmlisches Einbrechen, eine ganz unerhörte Tatsache: GOTT IST BIS ZU UNS GEKOMMEN UND HAT DAMIT DAS UNÜBERBRÜCKBARE ÜBERBRÜCKT.

Diese Brücke wurde vom Himmel her zur Erde geschlagen, und sie heißt Jesus Christus. Jesus Christus hat in eigener Person den tiefsten und letzten Wunsch des Menschen einmal und für immer verwirklicht, den Wunsch vergöttlicht zu werden und am Gottesleben teilzunehmen.

Die Kirche ist nichts als die bescheidene Treuhänderin dieser unbegreiflichen Botschaft. Und der Christ ist derjenige, der sich in schlichter „Naivität" entschließt, an diese Botschaft zu glauben.

Original:
Choisir sa religion
(Kairo/Ägypten 1971)

„Ihr seid Götter!"

Das Christentum ist die Religion des Menschen. Mit dem Christentum wurde in der Geschichte ein neues Zeitalter eröffnet – das Zeitalter des Menschen. GOTT IST MENSCH GEWORDEN ... , diese vier Worte haben den Sinn von Religion und Geschichte ganz verändert, obgleich noch keineswegs allen Menschen dieses christliche Zentralgeheimnis voll bewußt geworden ist.

Die Inkarnation bedeutet das Einsinken Gottes ins Innerste des in sich begrenzten Menschen. Sie vollzieht und verwirklicht die definitive Anwesenheit Gottes im Menschen und zwar vollständig und bis zur Einswerdung mit ihm. Die Menschwerdung Gottes war demnach eine Hochzeit, Gott und Mensch leben nun im Ehebund miteinander, d. h. sie sind eins geworden für Zeit und Ewigkeit. Das Unendliche Gottes floß ein in das Endliche der Kreatur, die Liebe Gottes erfüllt den Menschen – ganz.

Die Inkarnation war zunächst aber der Ausganspunkt einer „unvorstellbaren" Fortschrittslinie gewesen, der Beginn einer geistigen Evolution. Wohin wird diese den Menschen bringen? Welches Ziel verfolgt sie? Und wird es irgendwann einen Endpunkt auf dieser Entwicklungslinie geben, an dem wir unser Werden einhalten und alles zum Stillstand kommt? Wann wird das geschehen, wann werden wir „reif" sein? Und geschieht dieses unablässige Streben denn im Einklang mit dem göttlichen Willen, mit seinem Plan für Mensch und Welt, oder ist es unsererseits Vermessenheit, Trotz, Größenwahn? Richtet sich Wissenschaft und Fortschritt nicht gegen den Ordnungsplan der Natur und die Schöpfung, also gegen Gott? Fordern wir Gott nicht in blasphemischer Haltung heraus, wenn wir immer weiter vorrücken und fort-schreiten ..., „fort" von Gott? ...

Andererseits sagte Christus, daß wir jetzt zu allem befähigt wären, seitdem Gott sich in ihm der Menschheit verband, und daß wir noch größere Wunder vollbringen werden als er.

Also glaube ich an den Menschen und an seine Vernunft, weil ich an Gott glaube und an sein Wort; ich glaube an den Menschen, wie ich an Gott glaube. Glaubte ich nur an Gott allein, ohne an den Menschen zu glauben, dann dürfte ich mich nicht Christ nennen, denn das Christentum ist die Religion des Menschen, weil Gott seit der Inkarnation den Menschen bewohnt. Gott hat sich mit dem Menschen vermählt, d. h. er hat sich aufs tiefste mit ihm vereinigt, und diese Ehe ist unauflöslich. Gott hat den Menschen mit seinen eigenen göttlichen Kräften durchstrahlt, damit er Anteil an ihm habe.

Ich und der Vater sind eins ...
Ihr seid Götter!

(Johannes 10, 30 u. 34)

Deshalb darf man sich sagen:

„Weil Gott Mensch geworden ist, bin ich Gott geworden, denn Gott kam zu mir und lebt in mir. Seine Allmacht ist in mir, die Fülle seiner Kraft und seiner Weisheit steht mir zur Verfügung."

In dieser Hinsicht ist das christliche Mysterium ein revolutionäres Mysterium, Christ sein bedeutet eine revolutionäre Kraft sein, es bedeutet Manifestation einer neuen Wahrheit für Welt und Geschichte. Unsere Welt erwartet vom Menschen noch mehr als das, was Christus uns schon demonstrierte, „noch größere Wunder" hat er prophetisch vom Menschengeist vorausgesagt. Nein, noch längst nicht ist der Mensch zu seiner vollen Blüte gelangt.

ICH BIN DER WEG, DIE WAHRHEIT UND DAS LEBEN ... Dieser Weg, diese Wahrheit und dieses Leben werden uns eines Tages in ein ungeahntes Zauberland eintreten lassen! Gott selbst ist Achse und Fortschritt aller Geschichte, Gott in Christus und Christus im Menschen! Der Heilige Geist ist der bis ins Herz des Menschen erweiterte Christus. „*Wachst! Füllt! Mehrt! Schafft! Werdet!*" – das war das erste Wort Gottes an die sich bildende Menschheit, wie wir es im Garten Eden hören, denn die Grundlage aller Moral ist der Appell: „*Wachst und werdet!*" Alles Tun und Denken des einzelnen ist in diesen Strom hineingenommen, der die Welt in einem bestimmten Maße tatsächlich ansteigen läßt. Durch mein persönliches Handeln befolge ich das erste Gottesgebot. Und die Messe ist dieses Leben der Welt, das sich langsam fortschreitend wandelt, um einzumünden in Gott und dort in ihm seine Vollendung zu finden. Die Meßfeier ist die Feier der Wandlung.

Ich glaube an diese lebendige Kraft, die in der Menschheit lebt und wirkt und sich ständig mehrt. Ich glaube an die Kraft des Guten, und ich bin überzeugt, daß diese Kraft ansteckend ist! Ich weiß, daß das Gute ständig am Wachsen ist und daß es das Böse überwinden wird. Die Verachtung, Geißelung, die Kreuzigung, die Beweinung und die Grablegung Jesu, all das endete mit seiner Auferstehung. Unsere Menschheit muß in der Nachfolge den gleichen Weg gehen, auch er führt durch finstere Zonen dem Licht entgegen. Auch die Menschheit wird auferstehen!

Daher nennt man den gläubigen Christen einen optimistischen Menschen. Er bleibt Optimist – trotz allem! Sein Glaube besiegt die dunklen Mächte, die Widerstände gegen das Gute und selbst den Tod. Die christliche Zuversicht trägt ihn über alles hinweg, sie ist unzerstörbar. Ich glaube, daß der Mensch gut ist, weil die göttliche Liebe in ihn einzog und Keime setzte in seinem Innern. Das neue Herz, das Christus ihm schuf, wird sich eines Tages zu erkennen geben und auswirken im Sieg des Lichtes.

Es wundere ihn nicht, sagt Charles Péguy, daß der Glaube darin besteht, an das zu glauben, was ist. Auch die Liebe und Nächstenliebe lieben das, was ist. Hoffnung und Zuversicht aber, das wundere ihn, glauben an das, was nicht ist, und sie lieben bereits das, was noch nicht ist. In dieser zuversichtlichen Erwartung wird das Neue geboren, durch die Hoffnung wird es ans Licht gebracht, sie läßt das Unsichtbare sichtbar werden. In seiner Dichtung „Das Mysterium der Hoffnung" besingt Péguy in hymnischer Weise das kleine Mädchen Hoffnung oder diese kleine, starke, unauslöschliche Flamme Hoffnung:

> Sie ist es, die Kleine, die alles mit fortzieht.
> Denn Glaube sieht nur, was ist.
> Sie aber sieht, was sein wird.
> Liebe liebt nur, was ist.
> Sie aber liebt, was sein wird ...
> Die Hoffnung sieht das,
> was noch nicht ist und sein wird.
> Sie liebt das, was noch nicht ist und sein wird.
> In der Zukunft der Zeit und der Ewigkeit.
>
> (Charles Péguy)

Auch ich glaube an Euch, meine lieben Freunde! Zuversichtlich glaube ich an das, was Ihr noch nicht seid. Glaubendes Vertrauen sieht mehr, es schaut, was in der Wesenstiefe „an-wesend" ist. Jemanden lieben, heißt, ihn jenseits seinerselbst zu sehen und zu lieben, es heißt, das zu lieben, was er noch nicht ist, was er jedoch mit Sicherheit werden kann und werden soll und werden wird.

GLAUBEN, LIEBEN, HOFFEN UND VERTRAUEN – all das ist s c h ö p f e r i s c h e s T u n , denn es entfaltet, es bringt zum Sein.

Ich glaube an die Menschheit, sie wird werden! Und sie wird wunderbar werden! Eines Tages wird der Mensch wirklich im vollen Sinne Mensch geworden sein. Und dann wird er zugleich Gott sein. Schon heute darf er sich sagen:

Ich bin eine inkarnierte Gottesidee.
Ich bin ein Willensakt Gottes, der Form annahm.
Ich bin ein Liebesakt Gottes, der Fleisch annahm.
Ich bin ein Traum Gottes, der Wirklichkeit wurde.

Original:
Vous êtes des dieux! – Incarnation et progrès humain
(Kairo/Ägypten 1972)